Finding Your Soulmate

The Blueprint to How to Find Your Soulmate Even if Your Dating Life is Nonexistent.

By Christopher Conway

FINDING YOUR SOULMATE

FINDING YOUR SOULMATE

FINDING YOUR SOULMATE

© COPYRIGHT 2021 - ALL RIGHTS RESERVED.

The content contained within this book may not be reproduced, duplicated, or transmitted without direct written permission from the author or the publisher.

Under no circumstances will any blame or legal responsibility be held against the publisher, or author, for any damages, reparation, or monetary loss due to the information contained within this book. Either directly or indirectly.

Legal Notice:

This book is copyright protected. This book is only for personal use. You cannot amend, distribute, sell, use, quote, or paraphrase any part, or the content within this book, without the author or publisher's consent.

Disclaimer Notice:

Please note the information contained within this document is for educational and entertainment purposes only. All effort has been executed to present accurate, up-to-date, and reliable, complete information. No warranties of any kind are declared or implied. Readers acknowledge that the author is not engaging in the rendering of legal, financial, medical, or professional advice. The content within this book has been derived from various sources. Please consult a licensed professional before attempting any techniques outlined in this book.

FINDING YOUR SOULMATE

By reading this document, the reader agrees that under no circumstances is the author responsible for any losses, direct or indirect, which are incurred as a result of the use of the information contained within this document, including, but not limited to, — errors, omissions, or inaccuracies.

YOUR FREE GIFT

Finding Your Soulmate Tips Sheet

Sometimes you need a quick tip for a situation. This tips sheet points you to the best resources to help you fast!

(Get Yours Now...It's FREE)

Request FREE Tips Sheet Today. Go to:
https://loveblueprints.com/soulmate-tips-sheet/

TABLE OF CONTENTS

Introduction………………………………...**Page 10**

Chapter 1: PREPARING YOUR MIND & SOUL TO ACCEPT LOVE
....**Page 20**

Chapter 2: 'ATTRACTIVE-DEMONS' THAT YOU SHOULD AVOID AND WHY THEY CAN NEVER BE YOUR SOULMATE
....**Page 38**

Chapter 3: THE BEST WAYS (AND PLACES) TO MEET YOUR SOULMATE
....**Page 57**

Chapter 4: WHAT TO DO IF YOU MEET YOUR SOULMATE AT THE WRONG TIME IN YOUR LIFE
....**Page 76**

Chapter 5: SIGNS THAT YOU HAVE MET YOUR SOULMATE
....**Page 93**

Chapter 6: HOW TO MAKE LOVE WORK FOR YOU
....**Page 111**

Chapter 7: HOW SEX PLAYS A ROLE IN KEEPING YOUR SOULMATE
....**Page 129**

Chapter 8: WHY FINDING YOUR SOULMATE DOES NOT GUARANTEE THE RELATIONSHIP WILL LAST LONG
....**Page 147**

Conclusion
....**Page 165**

Your Free Gift
....**Page 172**

More Books by Christopher Conway
....**Page 173**

Reference List
....**Page 174**

INTRODUCTION

Being lonely is not a pleasant experience. Trust me; **I know how you feel, so let me help you experience happiness**.

Oh, lest I forget, it is the happiness that comes from having someone special to hug, kiss, and do kinky things with.

You wake up each night, rollover, and wonder if the love of your life will ever be sleeping next to you. Is it your destiny to find your soulmate, or are you cursed to only date mediocrity?

Bad feelings over past relationships might linger, causing you to feel emotional depression occasionally. Even with the avalanche of relationship advice out there, it may still feel like nothing works for you.

What if today you have the solution in your hands? The question remains- will you use it?

There truly is a blueprint to finding your soulmate. It's not posted online for free; otherwise, everyone would have it and utilize it. This blueprint is in your hands if you will only open it and follow the actionable steps.

Say goodbye to finding a date on your own or asking friends and family to set you up with someone. The entire process should start with you. It's not complex; nor is it beyond your abilities.

What you need to do and how you should approach this self-preparation process for finding your divine love are exclusively and explicitly detailed in this blueprint you now have in your hands.

The journey to finding your soulmate starts with preparing your mind and soul to accept love. You must also know the types of people you should avoid, followed by a series of steps to find your soulmate *(or have this person find you)*.

Sprinkle in knowledge to identify signs that you have met your divine love and your life sails towards everlasting love. You will also learn the secret of sustaining a newfound love interest and how to maintain a balance between physical and spiritual connection.

True, there are several books available claiming to help with finding a soulmate.

The problem with most of these books is that they

are just details of someone's love story. The story may be interesting, the plot captivating, but you are left wanting actionable steps towards finding divine love.

Those personal love stories are nothing more than a touch of erotica wrapped with spirituality. They're one person's story of how they found their soulmate, and maybe you can do the same, IF you are just like them, but you are unique. They tell you to *'manifest'* your soulmate, and *'poof,'* they will appear.

I can assure you that your life and view of relationships might be vastly different than those authors. If you're an action-taker with achievements under your belt, you already know that thinking and believing never makes a miracle come true.

Merely doing what those authors did may not yield the results that you want. You already know that to get what you want out of life; you must take the proper steps and avoid pitfalls.

What you need is the proper mindset and steps used by thousands who found their soulmates. That is what I give you in this program, and that is why you will love this one.

I have compiled the actionable steps and mindset shifts used by couples who found their divine love. Use this blueprint, follow the steps, and find your soulmate quickly.

Why You Need to Use This Program

Just imagine your life full of the happiness you've been dreaming about since you were a teenager. Imagine a life where you experience daily love from someone that shares your belief system.

This person can almost finish your sentences. They feel pain when you feel it and look for ways to make that pain go away. And you happily do the same for them— no more mental or physical loneliness.

You wake up daily to their smile, and right away, you know your day will be nothing but joyful. You hurry to complete your daily tasks at work because you can't wait to get home and see your soulmate again. Isn't that what you've been dreaming about night after night?

As you digest this program, take time to ponder, not daydream, about following the simple steps highlighted and how you can put them into practice. If you've been doing something the wrong way before now, *'empty your cup,'* so to speak, start doing things the correct way. You will benefit from it if you understand the points therein instead of rushing through everything.

Here is something else you can do: after each *chapter (carefully written to solve one problem at a time)* -- work at implementing the lessons from that chapter before moving on to the next. Then you can track your progress and be sure that you've benefitted from this program.

As you go through this program, you will realize that true love involves several little things that might be important to the other person, which you may not count as significant.

You will also learn how to transition from the *'honeymoon'* phase of a new relationship to the *'making it work'* phase, where conflicting views and disagreements may threaten your peace of mind.

You will also get to learn about love languages and why they are essential in a healthy relationship.

Here are positive reviews from readers:

"After reading just the first 12 pages of 'Finding Your Soulmate,' I knew this program would be a winner. No woo-woo fluff like most books. Just pure actionable steps to finding your soulmate."

Edgar Stark – Cape May, NJ

"Thanks for your advanced copy. Finally, a blueprint that shows you the steps to finding true love, not some think, and he/she will find you nonsense."

Bethanie Silverman – McCall, ID

As you have seen, my concern is not just publishing *'any'* kind of love program but giving people what can add real value to your quest for true love.

My Promise to You About Finding Your Soulmate

What do you stand to benefit from after reading this fascinating *'soulmate blueprint'*? When you complete this blueprint, you will have the mindset and actionable steps to go into the world to find your soulmate or have your soulmate find you.

Not only will you have the skillset to find your love, but you will also have techniques to position yourself to be discovered by your divine love. You will gain confidence and readiness to find love, and you will have mastered the art of sustaining a relationship even when confronted with the *'unexpected.'*

You will have reduced emotional stress while enjoying your night's rest, and depression out of loneliness will be alleviated. You will also be poised to help others find their soulmate.

You see, it is like getting two products for the price of one- you will help yourself and those who are willing to listen to you.

Why You Cannot Wait Any Longer to Use this Blueprint

To be blunt- you are not getting any younger. The clock is ticking, and each day that goes by, you lose an opportunity to meet your soulmate. Scare tactics? Well, yes, because it is true. Don't be so gullible in believing that love will come to you when you are not looking for it.

Motivational speakers can make you lose that sense of urgency, claiming that *'love is what happens when you are busy with other things.'* While it is not impossible, it rarely happens.

Take, for instance, someone who wants a job. Will this person wait for a job, or will they look for it? You'll agree that they need to look for a job if they don't want to remain unemployed. So waiting for love to happen is not a good strategy.

It's now time to re-orientate your mindset about love. Finding your soulmate is more than mere fantasy. You must set out to 'find' love. Instead of believing that love 'just' happens, why not start accepting the reality? The reality is that attraction can happen at any time. Understand that attraction is not the same as love.

You Need to Act Before that Attraction Can Lead to a Conversation

You also need to **act** before that conversation can lead to a regular conversation. And before an ordinary conversation can lead to an emotional attachment, you also need to **take more action.** You do not want to appear desperate because someone might quickly feel they can take advantage of you.

As long as you believe the widespread fallacy that love happens, the possibility of finding your soulmate is reduced daily. Be determined to change that mindset today and make that decision without delay. I don't want you to remain single against your will longer than you planned to. I am sure you don't want that either.

Work on your mood, be happy and be propelled by positive vibes. Happy people attract happy people. If you don't work on yourself, your chances of finding a soulmate might get cut in half.

If you occasionally struggle with depression, think carefully about the cause and what you can do to minimize such feelings. If you need to enlist the aid of a therapist, please do so.

Change your mindset if you have always believed in sexual gratification over platonic relationships. Remember that a good friend makes a better lover.

So be interested in building genuine friendships and not just looking for sexual attraction. Learn to differentiate between attraction, lust, and true love.

What You Should Know About This Blueprint

I know that you are ready to learn the 'how', the 'what,' and the 'when' for finding love. While I am so anxious to share all those with you, too, there is something you must understand about finding your soulmate.

This blueprint also explains how a relationship's golden rule works. The golden law for relationship states: *"do unto your partner what they want done to them."* That contrasts with the known golden rule to treat others the way you want to be treated.

In relationships, treating your partner how you want to be treated can cause severe damage because how they want to be treated may be different from your idea of being a good person.

You will also learn how to make someone fall in love with you, not by coercing them but by silent persuasion. Each chapter starts with a small introduction to highlight crucial lessons embedded in the chapter.

This program cannot take into consideration every situation that you might find yourself facing. Apart from that, what is applicable in one country or region may not be acceptable in another part because cultural factors differ. So while I present general advice, it is left to you to personalize and apply each lesson.

How to Start the Process to Meeting Your Soulmate this Weekend

They say, *"what is worth doing is worth doing well."* The other part of that nugget is that what is worth doing is worth doing fast. Don't wait until summer or your next vacation before implementing the tips in this soulmate blueprint. This next weekend presents an opportunity for you to start finding your special someone.

The weekend is a great time to start because people are more likely to meet and relate more on weekends. Weekends also present an opportunity for a more relaxed atmosphere, away from weekday hustles and stress.

People generally unwind and feel calmer on weekends than during business days. So, learn the secrets of finding your soulmate and unleash your new ideas on the weekend.

It is time to transform your life. Start using the actionable steps in this blueprint this weekend to find your divine love *(or have them find you)*. Do a favor for a friend and tell them about this program or buy it for them. Do not keep this valuable information all to yourself. Remember, read to understand, and do not rush over each of the topics. It will be a journey, and I will be your tour guide!

See you on the inside!

CHAPTER 1: PREPARING YOUR MIND & SOUL TO ACCEPT LOVE

Just as you need to cultivate a piece of land before crops can grow on it, the mind and soul need to be well-prepared to accept love. In this chapter, you will learn how to get ready for finding your soulmate.

You will know why it is essential to let go of any lingering past negativity and understand what you want in a potential soulmate.

Impact of Negative Thoughts

Negative thoughts will only bring negativity. We can all cultivate love, and we are all loveable. But your past negative experiences will want you to believe that no matter how much you try again, the result will not be any different from how it turned out the last time.

The past affects how the mind thinks and how we emotionally react to certain situations. It can even worsen if your brain subconsciously tries to make up for one's failures in a past relationship. What if your past love has caused you great emotional harm, and you feel you must get back at them?

Here is what Dr. Rhodes, a psychologist, and a dating coach, said:

> *"Our childhood experiences with our parents and our teachers and our friends do have a pretty big impact on how we operate both personally and professionally in early adulthood."*

As you try to avoid bad past experiences and work around any insecurities, it may reduce your chance of finding love again. To successfully find your soulmate, you must first learn to let go of past relationships and any pain those relationships caused.

What Could Be Holding You Back From Love

How will you know if you are still holding on to negative energies from past relationships? Here are some warning signs:

Making comparisons

If your past relationship is the yardstick for finding a soulmate, that is a clear sign that you may still be holding on to lingering thoughts from your past.

You might feel a need to find someone new but may want every detail about this new person *(how they look, how they smile, how they express love)* to be patterned after a past relationship.

Realize that two people are not the same, and no two relationships will be the same. These kinds of comparisons will hold you back from finding love because if your search does not produce something more like your past relationship, you will find it difficult to express love with someone new.

Living in a fantasy world

While there is nothing wrong with fantasizing about what you desire, if you continuously fantasize about a past relationship, that is another sign that you may still be holding on to the past.

If you always dream about sharing a warm embrace with a past love, having dinner with them, or going on a vacation with them, slow down a little and pay attention to yourself. You are not ready for a relationship. Spend more time letting go before inviting someone new into your life.

Talking about your past relationship

What a person talks about reflects what is in their heart. Do this now: think about how often you talk about your ex or your past relationships.

What is your answer? Often? More often than necessary? Or rarely? How you respond to this question determines if you are mentally ready for a new relationship or not.

If *'often'* and *'more often than necessary'* are one of your answers, it is a warning sign that you may still be holding on to the past. If you are holding onto past relationships, you will try to twist conversations with someone new towards your ex.

Doing this will only chase a new person away. This person will start to show less interest in you because people know when your focus is not on them but instead on someone else.

Keeping pace with your ex

You may claim to be over a past romance, but your actions show something different. You constantly research your ex online, maybe on social media or any other means available.

You feel as if it is your right to know everything about your ex, the same way you did when you two were together.

While this 'spying' may seem fun and worthwhile when you are bored, it is another warning sign that you are still holding on to a past relationship.

You may get hurt investigating your ex, only to discover that this person has moved forward with their world and not thinking about you anymore.

Wanting to get back at your ex

If you still feel like getting back at your ex, either for an affair or over another thing, that is a bad sign. It is an indication that you are still not over your former relationship.

You will bring that angry energy around new people that you meet. People can feel your anger, and when someone feels your anger, they become less interested in you.

Sure, they might not tell you. At first, someone new seemed interested, but their interest will fade after a few minutes, and you will not be sure why. The anger inside you will always chase away new love.

Brewing over hurt feelings

Okay, so you've had a negative experience with an ex. Perhaps it was emotional or physical abuse. Maybe it was the depressing effect of hurtful words, or maybe what hurt you was their infidelity.

If a considerable amount of time has passed since the incident and you are still fuming over what happened, it may be a cue that you are still not over that relationship.

This issue is different than just being angry. It's about pitying yourself. Oh, *"poor me,"* you say to yourself. *"I am sick of people doing bad things to me,"* you scream inside your head.

It would help if you stopped pitying yourself as the victim. A victim mentality does not attract love; it repels love.

Getting Over Negative Thoughts & Past Relationships

If you are still holding on to negativity from past relationships, understand that finding a soulmate will be a difficult thing to do. Now is when you want to prepare your mind for new love by getting over past negative feelings.

If you do not, this will negatively impact new relationships because you will be extra cautious about expressing your intentions and interests. Apart from that, you may criticize new people you meet because of unrealistic comparisons to your past.

Think about how they will feel knowing that someone from your past has a significant influence over how and what you do?

This outside influence will not help a new relationship grow! Instead of dealing with this type of situation, do not create this type of problem at all. Do whatever you can to move away from a negative past before starting any new relationship.

If you have thoughts about reconciling with your ex, realize that the chances are very slim. In the likelihood that you think you can repair your past relationship, understand that the problems you had before will resurface, whether you like it or not. Remember the cliché phrase, *"a leopard does not change its spots."*

Trust me; you do not want to return to a relationship that will give you neither joy nor love. Live in the present and not in your past thoughts. Believe that you are lovable even if your ex made you feel that you were not. Work on building your confidence.

If you want to build your confidence, speak with your friends, and ask them how they feel about you. It's reassuring to know that they appreciate you and enjoy spending time with you.

That way, you will know that **only** your ex felt differently about you. Next, do all you can to be as generous and hospitable to other people. Please don't do it because you want others to speak well of you, but because you want your actions to be the **new you.**

The point is that when you **know** that you can contribute real value to the lives of others, your confidence grows that you have value. Be happy with your life and with the decisions that you make.

Realize that splitting with your ex was the best possible decision you could have made at the time instead of brewing over being single. Avoid knowing too much or following what your ex Is doing in their life. The less you know about your ex's current life, the better for you.

While you may not need to delete your social media accounts, never search through social media because of curiosity about what your ex is doing. Get past the urge to track their life.

The less you know about your ex's current life, the easier it will be for you to start a new life without them.

Once you develop beyond your past relationship, then you can claim readiness to find your soulmate. Do you think these steps are doable? They are simple things you can do, but if they seem overwhelming, try this instead.

Take each task one step at a time instead of trying to implement everything at once. Believe that you can move past negative feelings and have an open heart to find your soulmate.

But that's not all you must do to get ready; you need to understand what you want in a new relationship.

A Proper View of Past Relationships

They say that every disappointment is a blessing in disguise. That is true of a failed romance because even though it hurts, there are many lessons to learn. Take a moment to ponder about your past relationships in order to itemize the following:

- What were the high points of the relationship?

- What memories will you want to keep?

These two questions will help you identify what you want to hold on to in your next relationship. Next, give careful thoughts to the following questions:

- When and how did the relationship turn sour?

- What mistakes did you make, and what should you have done differently?

- What did your ex do to hurt you?

Answers to these questions can help you to identify what you need to start doing differently in your new relationship. It will also help you know what can hurt you and what you need to change about yourself in order to not hurt your new partner.

The point is that you need to learn from failed past relationships instead of brewing over what occurred. Remember, what's happened has happened, and you can't turn back the hands of time.

However, you can use your past relationship as a stepping stone to achieving something more significant in the future.

As mentioned earlier, you need to get over a past relationship before moving forward to find your soulmate.

Have a Clear Vision of What You Want in Life

The next thing you must do to prepare your mind for a soulmate is to identify your goals.

- What do you want out of life?
- What type of person are you?
- What interests you, as well as irritates you?

Your answer to these questions reveals something interesting about you. These facts indicate what you want out of life and should influence your choice of a soulmate.

Maybe you used a past selection process that did not consider your answers to the questions above. Just choosing someone because they are attractive and have a cool or sexy 'style' usually ends with feeling as if you did not get value out of the relationship.

One day beauty fades, and someone's cool or sexy 'style' becomes irrelevant. That once physically attractive person may start developing wrinkled skin and a less beautiful body. When this happens, nothing else will matter except your desire for appreciation and companionship.

So, ask yourself again: *"what do you want from life?"* If you successfully identify what you want from life, it will not be hard for you to find someone who wants the same so that you reach your goals.

There are cases when the person you find attractive may not share your view of career, parenting, caring for in-laws, and health. They may even share a different idea of being successful. What about 'simple' decisions like where to live, vacation options, type of employment, and relationships with people?

These differences can result in serious conflicts, which can later cause heartaches and even breakups. Is that what you want in a relationship? I'm sure you do not! It is more critical than ever first to identify the things you want out of life.

As you complete this self-examination, the outcome prepares you to enjoy life with your soulmate. It also helps you see that choosing a soulmate goes beyond physical appearance and becomes more about what that person *'brings to the table.'*

Many can't find their soulmate because they don't know what they want out of life. If you fall into that category, understand that you are not alone.

More than 50% of people looking for a soulmate are clueless about what they want from life. It is never too late to define the values that you appreciate in life. So what can you do?

Please take a moment to think deeply about

where you would like to see yourself in, let's say....5 to 10 years. Ask yourself the following questions:

- Where would you like to live?
- What places do you want to visit?
- How would you like to handle finances?
- How large of a family do you want?
- If health issues come up, what type of treatment would you want?

Your detailed answers to these questions will help you understand what matters to you in life. If you can answer these questions with specificity, you have just increased your chance of meeting your soulmate.

Ensure that you determine how the other person feels about these critical matters early in your next relationship before committing to the relationship.

Preparing for Your Soulmate by Knowing Yourself

Is there something special that someone should know about you that drives your happiness? This *'something special'* is not about your goals or how you view certain matters in life. It is about the characteristics that define you as a person.

Why is this important? Because if you know

yourself, you will know who can help you be a better person and who is capable of bringing out the worst in you.

Wondering how to do this? Ask yourself these soul-searching questions:

- What do you love doing?
- How do you spend your free time?
- What legacy do you want to be left when you are gone?
- What mistakes are you prone to make?
- How do you view others?

Asking these series of questions will help identify what makes you happy, sad, stressed, and fulfilled.

You can also buy a journal and jot down daily your reaction to the negative actions of others. You could do this exercise for a month and study the pattern. Daily, for a month, you can also list how you react to positive things you experience. This simple exercise will help you identify various facets of your emotions and how you respond to them.

Let's say that you notice that you are prone to react negatively to certain situations. In that case, it is best to work at controlling your response to negativity because controlling your emotions is vital to managing a healthy relationship.

Try to monitor your interests, temperaments, values, and activities. This personality assessment will help you get a clearer picture of who you are and how you react to good and bad news.

The final step to knowing yourself is to invite well-meaning family and friends to give you a sincere comment about who they perceive you to be.

Make sure you get only honest answers *(positive and negative comments)* from them, as you may not be able to improve yourself without it. You may realize that there are things about you that you need to adjust or change completely.

Apart from your family and friends, you can also ask work colleagues or your boss to tell you what things they feel you can improve. Realize that they may tell you things that you know are serious personality flaws. Thank them and work at improving any undesirable traits that they pointed out.

Understanding What You Need in a Relationship

Identify your views

Relationships are give-and-take unions with both parties satisfying the desires of the other. It is symbiotic rather than parasitic.

Do not feel that you need to exhaust yourself to make the other person happy while you feel dejected and abandoned. You indeed want a soulmate, but you are not desperate. Good things come to those who consistently work towards their goals.

While we will discuss patience later in this program, let us discuss legitimate needs in a relationship and how to identify your needs. Many go into a relationship without specifying what they need from a relationship.

Let me walk you through the process of determining what you need in a relationship. Remember, this is not related to the other person; it's all about what you want.

Grab a piece of paper and honestly answer the following questions:

- Do you want kids? If yes, how many?
- Are you a jealous type of person? Why?
- What tolerance do you place on cheating and marital infidelity?
- How do you view divorce?
- How do you view expenses and investing, and how should they be handled in the relationship?

While a common law in physics says: *"like poles repel and unlike poles attract,"* the opposite is the case when discussing personal needs in a relationship. Shared values count the most.

Similar values act as cement that binds the bricks of a healthy relationship. When you identify what you want in a relationship, it will be easier to focus on someone as a potential soulmate who shares those same desires.

Emotional needs

While your views are essential, emotional needs are desires that easily define the relationship's mood, whether happy or sad. It is vital to identify your emotional needs before you can find someone who can fill them.

Like you did earlier, grab a piece of paper and honestly write down your answers to the following questions:

- How much sexual intimacy do you need?

- When you explain yourself, how much value do you place on being understood?

- What value do you place on respect and being honored?

- How do you handle constructive criticism?

- When you are sad, what things make you happy?

Your answers to these questions determine who can fill your need for being your ideal soulmate, someone who can cater to these emotional needs.

Identifying your love language

Your *'Love language'* refers to how you receive love from others. In other words, what others do drives you to feel loved.

The 5 love languages are:

- **Words of Affirmation**: Saying things that make others happy

- **Acts of Service**: Doing things that make others happy

- **Receiving Gifts**: Giving other people gifts to show you love them

- **Quality Time**: Spending time with them to show you appreciate their companionship

- **Physical Touch:** Being physically close to others often involves a measure of physical romance

Which love language makes you feel loved the most? Your love language is another thing you must know before expecting someone to fill it. Different things touch our hearts, and it is natural to have a different love language.

Understanding your love language is easy; all you must do is analyze your current relationships with family and friends. The acts that make you feel valued the most are your love language(s). Those actions are what you should expect shown to you by a potential soulmate.

Just like you need to pack your bags the night before you embark on a journey, finding your soulmate starts with preparing your mind for a social journey.

This chapter has discussed various points that can help you prepare for love. Never expect that your next relationship will heal all hurt from your last relationship. Some have waited for years preparing themselves for their soulmate.

Spend time reviewing your personality because that is what you are *'bringing to the table'* in your next relationship. Commit to being a more attractive version of yourself. Remember, happy people attract happy people. If you are a better person, your probability of attracting a better person will increase.

Once you are ready for love, you need to know the types of people to avoid if you want to find your soulmate. That's the subject of the next chapter.

See you there in the next chapter!

CHAPTER 2: *'ATTRACTIVE-DEMONS'* THAT YOU SHOULD AVOID AND WHY THEY CAN NEVER BE YOUR SOULMATE

This chapter focuses on the type of people you should never consider as potential soulmates. I call them *'attractive-demons.'*

You might think that the list is common-sense and that anyone with a brain should know to avoid these people. Well, when you feel love, sometimes common-sense goes out of the window.

I want to reinforce in you that you must avoid attractive-demons. It can be challenging to stay away from a person who is a terrible match for you when they possess traits you find attractive.

If you date them, these attractive-demons will mess up your life and leave you worse than before you met them. As we go through each category of demon, note why you should avoid them. Recognize that this step is vital towards finding your soulmate.

With most people, what you see isn't what you get. They might look nice, they might speak well, but when you take your time to get closer to them, you realize that you should have never dated them.

So far, you know how to prepare your mind and soul, but what good will that preparation do if the person you are considering isn't lifelong material?

Even when you date a 'good' person, relationships can be challenging. When the connection is to an attractive-demon, it can do you more harm than good.

Such relationships will eventually end, and when they end, you'll be left dissatisfied and frustrated. Of course, no one expects perfection from their partner, but ignoring the attractive-demon warning signs will leave you emotionally stranded.

Let us examine 8 categories of attractive-demons that you should never consider for a soul mate and why you should avoid them.

Attractive-Demon #1: Psychopaths

A psychopath can be a very charming person. This person can work a room like a social butterfly and draw all attention to themselves. However, under the cover lay someone with a personality disorder who exhibits manipulative patterns when others are not watching.

Another type of psychopath is someone with antisocial behavior. Be careful about interpreting the word 'antisocial.' People generally think that someone who is reserved or keeps to themselves might be a psychopath.

Anyone can be a loner or reserved and be socially well adjusted. The word 'antisocial' refers to someone who deliberately goes against societal rules or norms just for their satisfaction alone.

Here are common signs you may notice in a person that might be a psychopath:

- Careless disregard for the safety of others
- General irresponsibility
- Consistent distortion of the truth for personal gains
- Lack of empathy and emotions
- Inability to differentiate right from wrong
- Lack of remorse when guilty
- Consistent violation of the rights of others
- Always breaking the law

Other symptoms might be risk-taking, being verbally abusive *(not always physical)*, and impulsive.

Why is a psychopath wrong for you?

Not every psychopath will turn out as portrayed in American movies as serial killers and rapists. The majority lead everyday lives, away from the spotlight. You will eventually find yourself frustrated having to deal with their consistent irresponsibility. It is best not to date one in the first place because the relationship will have no future.

Consider the negative points I just mentioned that you would have to deal with and then ask yourself, *"Is this the life I want with a soulmate?"*

Psychopaths are pathological liars. A pathological liar will stop at nothing to conceal whatever they are trying to hide, regardless of who they must hurt or what story they need to invent. They try to get what they want from you, even playing the victim card if necessary.

They will have strategically planned stories to gain your pity and force you to yield to them. Eventually, you will grow tired of their manipulations, and the relationship will end. Psychopaths always feel hurt when their partner fails to bend to them or accept their ideas. A psychopaths' response to rejection is often rage.

A psychopath will attempt to manipulate you every chance they get so that they keep exerting control over you. What is alluring about psychopaths is that they show a remarkable ability to protect.

They are fearless in the face of danger and show strength. These are great traits that some even confuse for showing love.

Attractive-Demon #2: Narcissists

A narcissist is someone who thinks that their worth is more significant than its actual value. In other words, they admire themselves for delivering value that they have not indeed delivered. They believe that everything revolves around them, even their partners.

While it's not wrong to attach some measure of importance to ourselves, we must understand the actual value we provide to others and not over-state it.

Once we over-state the value that we provide to others, it can turn into a mental health condition known as Narcissist personality disorder.

Once you prepare your heart and soul to attract a soulmate, you will meet many people. If you meet someone and they exhibit any of the following characteristics, you just may have encountered a narcissist.

- A sense of importance that seems beyond the actual value they provide to others
- An excessive need for admiration and attention

- A general lack of emotions like empathy and mercy for people
- Unstable interest in things
- A 'me first' attitude as if no one else matters

Again, narcissists lead everyday lives, and they seldom maintain long-term relationships. However, their partners have had to put up with the humiliating emotional conditions just because they were afraid to start a new relationship.

They might have other charming traits. In the beginning, you might mistake their narcissism for confidence.

Why avoid a narcissist?

Here is a scenario that might occur: You are out together for dinner, and while enjoying a well-prepared meal, you engage in some constructive conversation. A narcissist will try to dominate the entire discussion, making everything revolve around themselves.

You may start a discussion and reference an event that happened to you in the past. A narcissist will often relate that situation back to themselves. A narcissist tends to take everything personal, especially if you fail to compliment them or praise them for something they feel is praiseworthy.

According to a medical report, deep down, they

loathe themselves; thus, they need adulations, admiration, and praise from people to remind them of their imaginary amazingness. When they don't get that constant praise, respect, and attention, they flare up and get angry.

Another sign of a narcissist is their tendency to talk badly about past relationships. Remember that narcissists take things personally. They will complain that a past love interest failed to deliver either constant praise, attention, admiration, or even respect.

As you listen to people speak, notice what they say about others. If they formerly adored someone but now condemn them, chances are one day; it might be you that they condemn.

Attractive-Demon #3: Control freaks

A measure of control is healthy. You need to control some things in your life and how you react to your environment. But when a need for control becomes extreme, a deep desire to control others' reactions makes one abnormal and freakish.

A control-freak feels that things will go out of control, or their lives may fall apart without the power to control.

Control-obsessed people may not see themselves as control freaks. Requiring control over everything in life is psychologically unhealthy because many things in life are beyond our control, especially another human.

How to know if a person is a control-freak

While we may exhibit the characters to be discussed from time to time, a control freak tends to exhibit these traits all the time. One thing that shows someone is a control freak is an eagerness to correct a person when wrong.

They find opportunities to correct others, either involving little things such as pronunciation and spelling. If they were witnesses to a mutual event, they would find a way to update the account with their version.

When they notice bad manners, they are always the first to point it out. If a toddler misbehaves, they are quick to scold the mother or guardian. What stands out is that they often want to tell you that you are wrong.

This is due to the underlying perception that they are always right. If you ever get in a relationship with someone like that, imagine how detrimental that will be to your freedom of speech.

Another sign someone is a control freak is their eagerness to have the last word in a discussion or a sustained tendency to win an argument. They try to set arbitrary rules in a relationship and argue for any reason.

They believe that they know more than others and are always right. Narcissists and control-freaks have lots in common. A control-freak is usually a narcissist, but a narcissist is not usually a control-freak.

Control freaks are known for criticizing others. They judge every action and speech that may not agree with what they believe to be correct. They are usually opinionated and feel that people should do things their way. They are always difficult to convince, especially when it is clear they need to change their view. With them, the word 'team' stands for 'me,' and 'us' stands for 'I.'

They find it easy to disagree with others just to do so, but they respond with rage and anger when others disagree with them. In most cases, control freaks are hypocritical. If you are trying to search for your special someone, avoid control freaks.

Attractive-Demon #4: People with personality disorders

Everyone has their personality, way of behaving, thinking, and feeling, making them different from other people. Certain factors can affect a person's character; factors like background, culture, genetics, and environment.

A person is said to have a personality disorder if they behave, think, and feel in a way that deviates from what is generally acceptable.

Of course, psychopaths, narcissists, and control-freaks have personality disorders. Their personality often causes problems for others, and it is offensive to many. If you want a soulmate, avoid people who are known to exhibit any of the following personality disorders:

- *Paranoid disorder.* This person tends to be unnecessarily suspicious of the intentions of others. They often mistake others' good intentions for evil motives, assuming people want to harm them.

- *Obsessive disorder.* They are obsessed with perfection and control. They pay too much attention to details and frustrate people around them.

- *Histrionic disorder.* These people feed on an excessive desire for attention. They are often clingy and nagging if not the center of attention. They can also become uncomfortable and jealous.

- *Dependent disorder.* They feel as if they cannot take care of themselves, thus excessively reliant on others. They find it hard to make simple decisions without help from others.

- *Borderline disorder.* They have unstable emotions and a poor self-image, needing constant reassurance from others. They have attempted suicide many times and are prone to self-injury.

- *Avoidance disorder:* They are extremely shy and often feel inadequate. When criticized, they feel hurt and are unwilling to mix and relate with people for fear of being rejected.

- *Schizoid disorder:* They often avoid social activities and find it hard to express normal human emotions.

Pursuing a relationship with any of the above-discussed personality traits will neither leave you satisfied nor fulfilled. The most reasonable thing is to avoid dating anybody with a known personality disorder.

Please note that some people may just be reserved and may not be suffering from any personality disorder.

Attractive-Demon #5: Momma's boy

How can I call a momma's boy an attractive-demon? Momma's boys are good men, kind and protective. Understand that dating them is no easy task because their mother controls their interaction with you behind your back.

What's the point of dating someone who is not ready to make decisions for themselves or tell their mother that she is wrong?

Falling in love with a momma's boy can be easy because of their kindness and concern for you. It's the same kindness and respect that their mother taught them to have for others. If you decide to carry on with such a relationship, expect the following:

- ***Undue comparison:*** They will often compare you to their mom. This comparison will be evident in small things like how you speak, act, clean, and even cook. You will experience many situations, telling you how their mother does things differently from how you just did it. Any attempt to convince them otherwise will fall on deaf ears because their mom is always right.

- ***Mom makes the decisions:*** Expect their mother's influence in any decision made. There is nothing that escapes mom's notice. Every time you both decide to do something, understand that mom already knew the issue before discussing it with you. There is a good chance that mom already decided, and the next move is to convince you that mom made the best decision.

Mom will constantly meddle in your affairs, and every disagreement will pass through mom's ears for her analysis. Mom will also know about your sex life and all the kinky things you like doing and done to you. Let that sink in for a moment.

- ***Less 'alone' time together.*** Expect a significant number of dinners, vacations, holidays, and cold days with mom as the third-wheel. Expect mom to tag along during a considerable number of these moments that you wanted to bond with your partner. It will feel as if mom is always there, and she won't be shy about expressing dissatisfaction with anything you do or say. It will be like walking on eggshells around her.

- ***Mother is always right / you're always wrong.*** If you disagree with mom, you can be sure that the momma-boy will take mom's side and not yours. It will not matter if mom is dead-wrong. If there is anything mom could be right about, that will be the focus.

- ***Competition with their mom:*** You should not have to beg or clamor for attention in your relationship. But with mom in the picture, you will have to jostle for attention and affection. Imagine talking to your partner on the phone, and their mom calls; your partner will end your call to speak with their mother.

There is another problem: your partner wanting things done their way, like a spoiled baby. Remember that mommas-boys were babied from infancy, and their mom always satisfied them. You can expect that same rotten attitude from your partner in your relationship.

How to identify a mamma's boy

- If mom shows up unannounced even with keys and just opens the door

- If mom tells your partner how to dress, buys them clothes, and underwear

- Their mom fixes their problems, work issues and meddled in their past love life

- Mom still does your partners' household chores and laundry

- If you check your partner's call record and mom shows up 7-times out of 10-entries

- If mom does not appreciate you no matter how much kindness you show her, she may be jealous of you for taking her place in her child's life

- If mom is wrong, but your partner finds it difficult to stand up to her

As earlier mentioned, mamma's boys are good people, but having to compete with their mom frequently is a warning sign for you not to start a relationship with such a person.

Attractive-Demon #6: A person with too many friends of the opposite sex

I must speak exclusively to straight-people in this

section. Some ladies prefer male friends. Understand one thing; men and women were not placed on this earth to be buddies. We were put on this earth to be sexually attracted to each other and have babies. That is our primal *(animalistic)* purpose in life.

Any male 'friends' that a woman interacts with feels either a romantic or sexual attraction for her. Either these guys want to date her long-term, or they just want lustful sex.

It's rare for any of these guys to want to be her brother figure or buddy. For this reason, if you date a woman with lots of male 'friends,' be prepared for these men to find fault in just about anything you do.

Any misunderstanding will be the guy up to evil. These 'friends' will seldom try to find ways to make the relationship stronger. Helping you build a stronger love works against their self-interest.

The same issues occur if a guy has too many lady friends. These lady orbiters want to find anything wrong with the woman in the guy's life.

If you start a relationship with a person who has too many friends of the opposite sex, it's like having too many hostile forces working against you.

These so-called 'friends' will hear about your relationship problems and offer solutions before you get a chance to influence the outcome. Is that what you want in a relationship?

You want a soulmate to give you the first opportunity to influence the direction of the relationship.

Attractive-Demon #7: Liars & Cheaters

At some point, we have all been untruthful, maybe to save face or to avoid troubles. However, liars are **ALWAYS** dishonest, aiming to deceive others just to stay safe. They have formed a pattern of lying, and people no longer believe them even when they attempt to speak the truth.

Cheaters are closely related to liars because their love interest never limits itself to you. When you see through them, they tell lies to get out of the situation.

Liars and cheaters are two categories of people you should avoid dating. For one thing, you will always doubt what comes out of your mouth; and not freely open to them. Love should be a free expression of your feelings.

Trust will also be hard to establish, and without trust, love cannot grow. You will always look for where their story doesn't add up because they have created a reputation for untrustworthiness. You want a love that you can relax into, not a love you must always doubt.

Here are warning signs that someone is a potential liar and/or cheater:

- They always hide their phone from you
- They never let you read their emails or messages on the phone
- Their story does not always add up
- They are found untruthful in little things
- They are known for flirting

If you notice several warning signs mentioned above in someone, you feel attracted to, save yourself the stress and avoid them.

Attractive-Demon #8: People who never admit their faults

Both parties must be ready to forgive the other for a relationship to thrive because it is easier to move past issues. To receive your partner's forgiveness, you must be prepared to admit your mistakes and apologize. A simple *'I was wrong'* or *'I am sorry'* can go a long way to soothe hurt feelings.

What if you are with someone who never accepts their mistakes? They believe that you are wrong, and they are always right! No matter how much evidence, they dogmatically insist that they are right and thus see no reason to apologize.

A failure to admit fault can put lots of strain on your relationship. It can even lead to breakups because if the situation persists, you start feeling less confident about your worth and abilities.

Even when you know you have done your best; you still doubt your value. Just like with narcissists, an inflated feeling of superiority can be responsible for this. How will you know if the person falls into this category?

- When you make discussions with them, they insist on having their way
- When planning, this person never asks your opinion
- When they make mistakes, they justify their actions, perhaps shifting the blame
- Instead of apologizing when wrong, they remind you how lucky you are to have them
- They can't name a single thing that they did wrong in a past relationship

If you notice these traits, do not proceed with a relationship with this person. Avoid them because they can eventually ruin your self-image. In this chapter, I discussed the types of people you should avoid to find a soul mate. This step is challenging to follow.

People often hold back certain sides of their personality until you show your emotional commitment to them. At that point, your feelings may cloud any rational thought.

You must be strong to overpower your emotional feelings and get out of the relationship. Some may say that these personality types are clearly people to avoid, but now you have a checklist to refer back to as you date.

If the person you are considering falls within one or more of the personality types outlined, and you still move forward with the relationship, you can only blame yourself if things go badly.

Now that you know the types of people to avoid, you're ready to start the next step towards finding your soulmate; identifying ideal places you can meet your divine love.

Your divine love isn't going to pop out of your closet through some manifestation process. You're going to have to place yourself in front of humans, online and offline.

If you enjoyed this chapter about *'attractive-demons'* to avoid on your journey to finding your soulmate, you're going to love the next chapter about the best places *(and ways)* to meet your soulmate.

See you in the next chapter!

CHAPTER 3: THE BEST WAYS (AND PLACES) TO MEET YOUR SOULMATE

This chapter focuses on finding your soulmate once your mindset is ready to receive this person. You want to meet your special someone, but you cannot manifest this person with your thoughts alone.

You must put yourself in places to be discovered or where you can discover someone special. Must you attend every local event or join every online dating site before you meet them?

Well, not every local event and dating site, but as many as possible. I will touch on these methods because you must put yourself in the presence of people to meet someone special.

Understanding what you want in a soulmate

Finding your soulmate is not about finding just

anyone. Your soulmate must be willing and able to satisfy your emotional and physical needs.

Some say that finding your soulmate is about finding someone birthed who amplifies your strengths and plugs the holes of your weaknesses. So how can you know if the person you feel attracted to is this divine person?

You want to look beyond superficial traits. While someone may be attractive and charismatic, you still need to go through the soulmate checklist you established earlier.

It takes time to decipher the person hidden behind gorgeous looks. You must spend time with them over a couple of dates. You also want to observe how they relate with others because how they treat others will eventually be how they treat you.

Take an objective look at them to see what their actions reveal about them. Keep your soulmate checklist in your mind as you meet people.

I do not believe in allowing fate to hand you a soulmate. You find a soulmate when you know what you want, and your eyes remain open for when this person crosses your path. If unsure of what you want in a soulmate, here are few things to look for and why they are necessary.

Does this person believe in you?

Everyone has dreams and life goals. These aspirations guide most decisions that we make in life. The reason for this is that everything we do is tied to our life goals. Your soulmate choice should be someone that supports you as you pursue your goals in life and not someone that deters you or slows you down.

Your soulmate choice determines the success of reaching your goals. Imagine dating someone that views you as a medical assistant when you view yourself as a surgeon.

This person cannot be your soulmate because they view your career differently than how you view it. If someone does not believe that you can achieve as much or more than you believe you can achieve, this person is not your soulmate.

Your potential soulmate should be your number one fan. When you make a mistake, they will show you how to recover, not criticize you, which can lead to a loss of self-confidence. In your journey to find a soulmate, make sure that you find someone who believes in you as much or more than you believe in yourself.

What effect will they have on you?

Your soulmate should bring out the best in you. When you are sad, they should be the reason why you smile. When your confidence is low, they should be that silent cheerleader urging you to push forward. You want a partner who boosts your emotions.

If all you think about is bitterness and anger when together and if your best days are being alone, these are signs that such a person is not the right one for you. The same way you expect this person to bring out the best in you, you must also be capable of bringing out the best in them. You both should shine better when together.

Your soulmate should also be someone who tells you when you are wrong or going down the wrong path. You do not want someone who agrees with you all the time.

You cannot improve if someone does not tell you hard truths. Evaluate each person you find attractive and ask yourself: *'Does this person bring out the best in me?'*

Will they put a smile on your face?

Is it love if you are not smiling? First, you must be happy before you can meet your soulmate. Your soulmate should amplify your happiness, and a great indication of happiness is smiling when you see them.

When you open the door or hold a video chat, does the sight of their face make you smile? When you are with this person, the atmosphere should feel electric. Even if they are not naturally funny, their presence must be enough to make you smile. They should make you laugh, even when doing everyday things.

In their presence, you should feel free to be yourself; childish, playful, or serious. When you are in a bad mood, they take you out of that emotional dungeon and make you smile again. If they cannot do these things, your soulmate may still be somewhere waiting for you.

Are they reasonable in times of disagreement?

A reasonable person reacts sensibly during times of disagreement. Why should you expect a sensible soulmate? The reason is that every decision they make reflects on you.

Others will project your partner's actions onto you, and in most cases, judge you by them. There are times you may not be able to think clearly for one or more reasons. If your soulmate is sensible, they will be able to make wise decisions on your behalf.

A reasonable person understands the value of yielding or acquiescing when necessary. It may be a decision that touches both of your lives.

If your partner is stubborn and insistent, decisions may benefit your partner more than you. A sensible soulmate is ready to compromise without hurting you or making enemies.

Does this person respect you?

Respect is defined as admiration for someone

and their abilities or qualities. It can also be explained as due regard for the wishes of others or their rights. When learning about someone, notice how they react when you express your opinion.

Take mental notes of their reactions when you make a decision that is different from what they would have done. Your observations will indicate if they respect you or not.

Consider their trustworthiness

They say that once in a lifetime, someone will betray you. When that comes from someone close to us, like your partner, the scar never heals. Before you get too emotionally involved, study this person well before starting a relationship with them.

Do they give you reasons to distrust them? Do they hide their mobile phone and other personal information? Do you feel that they are dishonest when disclosing their finances?

These are indicators that you should not ignore. Trust is a two-way street, so if you expect trustworthiness, you should be trustworthy yourself. After love and respect, trust is often regarded as the third most crucial quality expected in a soulmate.

They should have a forgiving spirit

As imperfect humans, one thing is familiar to us

all: mistakes. If we do not stumble in actions, we stumble in words. When we offend, feelings get hurt, and tempers flare. If one does not course-correct quickly, grudges can fester and damage relationships.

Every relationship experiences occasional disagreements. It may be as a result of something said or done. It could also be a result of something not said or not done. It might also be a result of a difference of opinion. While disagreements are unavoidable, one thing can help you both pull through no matter the issue: forgiveness.

Forgiveness is the art of overlooking ones' unintentional error because we value the relationship with that person more than our ego. Notice that I said 'unintended' error.

If someone hurts you without knowing, it is vital to have a forgiving spirit. If you date the wrong person, they may hold every mistake you make against you. A person who lacks a forgiving nature uses a person's errors to control them.

When you forgive, you do not preserve the action in memory to use against someone later. When someone holds onto wrongdoings, they keep every hurt feeling in a mental ledger that they open in the future.

They remind you of your unintended mistakes to manipulate and control you. A person who lacks a forgiving spirit finds it challenging to let go of what happened.

Take a moment to consider the person you find attractive. Do they have a forgiving spirit? If you make mistakes, will they use those mistakes against you? In their past relationships, has this person shown forgiveness for unintentional errors? Your soulmate should have a forgiving spirit. The success of your relationship depends on both of you having forgiving hearts.

Does this person show gratitude and appreciation?

Appreciation builds bonds. When someone passionately thanks you for your actions, it makes you feel appreciated. A quick thank you is never enough.

Appreciation is when someone looks you in the eye, touches you on the shoulder or hand, and verbalizes their gratitude for what you have done for them. The act could be your words or a deed. This appreciation motivates you to do your best to make that person happy.

On the other hand, an ungrateful person will not passionately give thanks. They might say 'Thanks,' but without any emotion behind it. An ungrateful person does not feel the energy that went into the good deed done for them.

There was no transfer of energy from them to you. You can never bond with an ungrateful person; therefore, that person can never be your soulmate.

What evidence has the person you have your eyes set on displayed to show appreciation?

They know how to show love

Love is so many things. It is the engine that drives a relationship forward; the cement that binds two people together; and the shield against forces that might try to damage a relationship.

Anyone you think could be your soulmate must know how to love because they have done it before. How will you know if someone can show love?

Consider the following indicators:

- They were loyal in a past relationship. If they stood by that person through hell and heaven. If they defended that person in that person's absence. These are clear signs of someone who knows how to show love.

- They do not hide their negatives. They show comfort in sharing their lives with you and the things they are going through.

- They are willing to help you in practical ways. Even if this help does not benefit them directly, they are eager to lend a hand.

- They take care of others: family, friends, co-workers. They do what is in their power to help others turn a bad situation into a good or manageable one.

- They listen when you express your viewpoint, even if that viewpoint contradicts their own. You can feel that they heard your opinion, even if they completely disagreed with it.

When you find someone that checks off this entire list, your soulmate could be stirring at you. Never settle for anyone that does not possess all these qualities.

Finding love when you expect it

While love will not find you while sitting at home thinking about it, you never know when you will find it, or it might find you. It is romantic to say that true love happens when you least expect it because it makes for a great romance novel.

Many people say that they did not plan to meet their soulmate and that it just happened. This characterization gives you the impression that you can sit at home, never surround yourself with people, and poof, love finds you while sleeping on your couch one day.

Consider what certified life and relationship coach Kelli Fisher said:

> *"When you are focused on meeting someone, the stress can be seen from a mile away……. When you do not have that at the top of your mind and are just enjoying yourself at the moment without any preconceived notions, things can progress organically".*

Notice that she did not say to sit at home and think about love. She said to enjoy yourself while out in a social setting, then love can organically find you as you mix with people. Instead of focusing on meeting someone special every time you go to an event, focus on enjoying yourself.

Here are various things you can do that will place you in the company of people:

1. **Invest in your hobby**: We all have our hobbies. Maybe it is ice skating or going to the park to enjoy reading a novel. Whatever makes you happy, invest your time doing more of it to surround yourself with people.

   You should not invest in your hobby with the sole purpose of meeting your soulmate. You should do it to enjoy the activity. If your sole purpose is to meet a soulmate and you come home from each event not meeting this person, the disappointment can drain your energy.

2. **Make more friends**: If you enjoy meeting people, invest your time and resources in that. You could go camping with friends or hunting if that's what you love to do. You can meet other campers and hunters.

   Do you enjoy reading or watching movies? Join a local book club or movie club. There will be lots to talk about after the event. Ensure that you have a love for the hobby and not just going to the event to find a soulmate.

3. **Re-evaluate your relationship checklist:** You have a set of qualities that you want in a soulmate. Earlier in this chapter, we reviewed qualities that should be on your list.

   From time to time, it is vital to re-evaluate this list. Why should you do that? Our desires change as we grow older. What you wanted in a partner 5-years ago may differ from what you want in a soulmate today.

If you execute the steps outlined in this section, not only will you have more fun, but you position yourself to meet someone special. Focus on having fun at activities and let meeting your soulmate be a bonus.

I will give you many more ideas on where you can

meet more people who might be your soulmate. The more attractive you are as a person, the greater your chances of meeting someone when you least expect it.

Making a good first impression

The impression people formulate about you the first time they meet you never escapes their minds. Therefore, it is essential to make that first impression positive. Your first impression may be the key to unlocking that special moment when you meet your soulmate.

How can you make an excellent first impression? Here are a few ways to do it:

Dress and smell good

Please do not overlook the value of dressing well to find a soulmate. You do not need to wear tight clothing or show lots of skin.

Looking frumpy is not a good idea either. Regardless of your body's shape or physical weight, anyone can wear nice clothing that fits them well.

The point is that you want people to see you as someone who cares about themselves. Wear clothes with matching colors and patterns. Smell good with cologne or perfume, but not too much. One spray on the neck is all you need. Pay attention to your shoes and avoid color riots.

Be proud of where you are in life

Do not try to be someone you are not. If you are a high school teacher, say it with pride and not sadness in your voice. You attract the energy that you emit. If you want to attract a soulmate who has confidence, you must show confidence. Do not act rich when you are not.

Choose your words wisely

Be polite when speaking to others and compliment when appropriate. Let it show in your voice that you appreciate and value the opinions of others. When people are kind to you, express your gratitude generously and never be too shy to say that you are sorry when necessary. Your soulmate could be behind you, listening.

Talk about positive things in life; and not about how the world is screwed up; and that people are cruel; and that the government spends too much; and blah blah blah about the negatives in the world. You will only attract negative people to date, willing to complain as well.

Be mindful of your posture

Your posture says so much about how you view your life. You may not say anything, but your body language has a lot to say about you. When you speak to someone, they can tell if you have a passion for what you say.

Slouching is not an attractive look, and it only repels people. Even if your life is not going as planned, keep a positive posture to attract positive people.

Put your cellphone away when meeting people

If you speak to someone, you expect them to listen to what you say. When on your mobile device, people ignore you because you appear busy. When at events, you want to interact with people and look approachable.

To make an excellent first impression, put your phone away during conversations with someone. It shows that you value what someone has to say. Your soulmate might be the one speaking to you. It would be a shame if they viewed you as rude and walked away.

Trusting your intuition when searching for a soulmate

You might think that you do not have superpowers, but nature gave you intuition. There are times when you know something without being told or seeing anything. That is intuition, and many times, it is correct. Intuition involves listening to that inner voice as you analyze your next move.

Intuition is the highest form of individual brilliance because our innate feelings are usually correct. As you learn to harness the power of your intuition, you start to trust yourself more to make the right decisions.

There is another advantage of trusting your intuition. Intuition is always on your side, looking out for your best interest. Trusting your heart helps avoid unhealthy relationships with the wrong person. Here are things you can do to sharpen your intuition:

Avoid overthinking

Overthinking creates problems that do not exist and amplifies an issue beyond its current state. If you are not careful, this can negatively affect your intuition, causing it to give you mixed signals.

Let go of past trauma

Just as past traumas can change our outlook on life, it is vital to resolve in our hearts that we need to move on. If not, every intuition-trigger gets influenced by lingering thoughts of the past. When this happens, your intuition becomes less reliable.

Meditate more

Meditating frees your mind, taking your mind to a spiritual place. When you do not think rationally, spending time meditating will free your mind and reset your intuitive powers.

Pay attention to your body

What you feel influences your intuition. Control

your emotions and avoid negative feelings like sadness, anger, and resentment. As you examine how you feel, you will know the best time to allow your intuition to make individual decisions for you.

Places to meet your soulmate

You can meet your soulmate anywhere and at any time. There are several great but unexpected venues where you can meet your soulmate. While this list is not comprehensive, it lists familiar places where you people meet people.

Offline places

Remember that your soulmate will not magically appear if you only think; you must also do- act and get out of the house as often as possible.

- Your workplace – You are at work 8 hours a day, maybe more

- In your neighborhood – If you live in an urban area, you probably walk to the grocery store, the cleaners, etc.

- At school – You can sign-up for classes at a local college and participate in study groups

- In the airport / On the plane – If you travel for work often, be open to people at the airport

- The gym – This is a great place to meet someone who shares a passion for health

- Public transportation – Maybe you take public transit to work; be friendly to people you see

- Volunteer – If you love pets or care about the homeless, you can join non-profit groups

- Religious center – Attending church also puts you in contact with people, and you can volunteer

- Local investment club – Another great place to meet people and maybe your soulmate

In all these places, you are visible to others. Once you build an attractive personality and style, you are positioned for your soulmate to find you.

Online places

You can also find true love online through online dating apps. Some of the top dating sites are easily found by using Google. Search for *'top dating sites'* and get a complete list. You might feel that online dating sites are filled with strange people.

That might have been the case years ago, but today you find the same caliber of people online as you find volunteering at non-profit groups or work.

If people were honest, I would bet that 70% of the people you see in church, at work, in the grocery store- all have online profiles on some dating site. Most people will not admit this fact, but more people are dating online and finding their soulmate than you realize.

Just register and set up a profile. Upload the best photos of yourself because your first impression will be your smile, your face, and of course, your body shape. Regardless of your body, you can wear the best clothing you have that gives you the smoothest look.

Online dating is more advantageous to people in their 50s, 60s, 70s, and 80s. I bet you did not know this fact. People over 50 are more serious about finding their soulmates.

If you are in your 20s and 30s, online dating can be more challenging because many of these people are just looking for a good time, not necessarily a soulmate. If you are in your 40s, finding a soulmate online can be a mix of serious connections and fun-seekers.

If you enjoyed this chapter about the best places to meet your soulmate, you will love the next chapter about what to do if you meet your soulmate at the wrong time in your life.

See you in the next chapter!

CHAPTER 4: WHAT TO DO IF YOU MEET YOUR SOULMATE AT THE WRONG TIME IN YOUR LIFE

Timing can work for or against you.

Meeting your soulmate is an experience most people want to have. In fact, many people yearn to have that deep-seated connection with someone, where they are sure that they are soulmates, destined by the universe to be together for life.

The thrill is exciting. Your soulmate has a way of making everything seem right. When they are around, the skies suddenly seem brighter. Their smile is the center of your world, and although you may not like it, it draws you in, and you are content to stare at them all day long.

With your soulmate, the connection is almost instantaneous. They feel the connection deep within just as you do, and if you are to have your way, you would want to seal the deal and get married to them immediately.

Your soulmate's appearance is usually characterized by nothing short of joy, happiness, peace, and contentment.

Although everyone (including you) prays to meet their soulmate, there are some conditions when being with your soulmate is downright impossible (or close to impossible).

One of these conditions is when soulmates encounter themselves at the wrong time. Just as with every other thing in the universe, timing plays a significant part in the subject of love and whether a relationship between soulmates will eventually blossom.

Let's take a quick look at the concept of *'meeting your soulmate at the wrong time.'*

What does *'the wrong time'* mean?

Back when you were much younger, *'the wrong time'* could mean many things in different situations. It could mean that it was past your curfew or that your parents may not have had the resources to purchase your 'ideal' birthday gift for you at the time. In any case, whenever it was not the right time for something, you were not going to get it.

This is the same thing that applies to the concept of meeting with and getting together with your soulmate. Although there is no curfew for you to keep to, you are not under the watchful eyes of parents and guardians who constantly remind you to make nice. Meeting your soulmate at the wrong time will, in most cases, lead to a lot of longing, pining, and loneliness.

In a nutshell, *'the wrong time'* in this context implies that although you have met your soulmate, the timing is not yet right, and for some reason, you will not be able to pursue and sustain the kind of relationship you are looking to have with them.

What constitutes *'the wrong time?'*

Now that you know that it is possible to meet your soulmate at the wrong time, you are most likely asking the question, *'how do I know that it is the wrong time?'*

Answering that question lies in understanding what constitutes *'the wrong time.'* Here are a few classical situations where you know that you have met your soulmate at the wrong time.

A. *Your soulmate may already be married*

And this news can wring your fluttering heart right out of your chest.

Imagine this scenario: You have always been a romantic at heart since young. You sit on the couch with a bowl of popcorn and a bottle of soda all night long- watching movies where the protagonists always win that special someone after all the hurdles they go through.

The last scenes of these movies leave you with

butterflies in your belly and a glimmer of hope that you, too, one day, will be like the protagonists in the movie - you will find your soulmate and walk with them into your happy-ever-after.

Although your friends scold you for doing so, you cannot seem to stay long in a relationship if it doesn't feel right. Sometimes, you avoid relationships and casual meetups with prospective partners only because you are waiting for the right one to come into your life and sweep you off your feet.

One day, when you least expect, you meet 'the One.' You feel yourself get flustered at the sight of them because you fit yourselves perfectly and make each other feel whole, just like pieces of a jigsaw puzzle.

They brighten your world, and you may even catch yourself a few times as you daydream about a happy-ever-after with them.

Your hopes shatter when you discover one day over coffee that the person you are sure is your soulmate is already married.

Although you are convinced that they feel the same thing for you as you do for them, a part of you dies as you learn that they are already entangled with another person for life.

If you are not careful, there is a tendency that you may throw caution to the winds and get involved in something you should not. You may start having an affair with the person, and often, this decision is fueled by your soulmate's proclamation to leave their spouse to be with you.

Meeting your soulmate at this time is dangerous because the connection that follows can lead you down the wrong path of making terrible decisions or leave you in a state of longing, pain, and angst.

B. *Both of you may be fresh out of a bad relationship*

Not many people get out of a bad relationship to jump straight into a new one. And your soulmate may not make an exception because they met you.

When you meet your soulmate just after this person has just gotten out of a bad relationship, you may dislike them instantly. This is because although passion may exist between both of you, they may not be eager to pursue things with you.

Consequently, they may be nasty toward you, treat you with levity, or consciously get on your nerves. The reason for this is because they seek ways to get you out of their minds and maybe out of their lives for good.

They believe that if they can make you see them as a terrible person, you will dislike them, and your response toward them will change. They hope to take advantage of the dislike you will have for them to get you out of their minds and their hearts for good.

Although this may sometimes work, no rule says it must always work. However, meeting your soulmate at this time is hardly a walk in the park.

You may need to scale a lot of hurdles together, and whether both of you will be together ultimately dependents on the amount of work you are willing to put into the process of making things work.

C. Both of you may not be ready for anything "more"

"Someone can be madly in love with you and still not ready. They can love you in a way you have never been loved and still not join you on the bridge."

- Nayyiah Waheed.

Many people have at some point experienced this. After meeting with their soulmate and experiencing the thrills of finally getting to interact with the one for them, they get stumped because although they are sure the attraction is two-sided, their soulmate doesn't seem inclined toward pursuing anything more with them.

When you look deeper into the quote above, you will discover that it depicts another scenario when you can say that you have met your soulmate, but at the wrong time. This is arguably one of the most challenging *"wrong time"* situations because you may not be able to place a finger on the exact reason why your soulmate has refused to pursue anything more with you.

On the flip side, you may have met your soulmate - either professionally or personally. They may have come into your life as colleagues at work, a potential client you must work with, or just as a neighbor next door.

However, you may not be inclined towards them because you are not yet ready to be anything more than what you already are - platonic friends/acquaintances. This has happened to many people over time. In most cases, the result of this situation is that both of you may end up running around in circles for an exceptionally long time.

D. *You may be married already*

This is just in line with the last point above. Meeting your soulmate after when you are currently married can be a challenging situation. This is not entirely unusual as there have been many incidents when this has happened to people.

When this happens, you experience the sparks and emotional high that comes with meeting someone who completes you in all obvious ways. Being around them is comfortable and rejuvenating.

You feel the mutual connection, and if you do not handle this correctly, it can lead to many challenges simultaneously.

For one, you may be tempted to move with the tides. This implies that you may throw caution to the winds and succumb to having an affair with them, especially if your marriage was already experiencing some challenges before this time.

When you meet your soulmate at this time, it may be impossible for you to be with them.

What to do when you meet your soulmate at the wrong time

After understanding that it is possible to meet your soulmate at the wrong time, you must know how to handle this if it should happen.

Understand that timing is everything in the game of love

Although this line sounds like a typical cliche, it is the absolute truth. Timing is everything in the game of love. The same way your parents may not get you that present you want for your birthday because they do not have the financial resources to (it was the wrong time), you may meet your soulmate at the wrong time.

This is what we have spent the last section of this chapter discusses.

Love is fantastic, and everyone wants to meet that one person for them. However, this connection may not lead to a happy ending if it happens at the wrong time. There are a few reasons why timing is vital in love and establishing a genuine connection with your soulmate.

- ***Finding your soulmate at the right time is vital if you're going to end up with the person you love.***

    If the four scenarios discussed in this section are removed from the equation, you will discover that it can be straightforward to build an enviable relationship with your soulmate; once you meet them.

- ***Finding your soulmate at the right time ensures that you do not go through the emotional pain that accompanies not being able to be with the one you love, even after you have met them.***

    Before you meet your soulmate, there is this longing in your heart. You want to meet that person who the universe designed for you and feel that the puzzle pieces have slipped into place. Meeting this person at the wrong time will only cause this longing to increase.

Now that you know they are there, it may be difficult or borderline impossible to stay away from them, and often, this leads to a lot of pain and heartaches.

- *Meeting your soulmate at the right time is necessary if you do not want to make a mistake that you might regret.*

    Many people who have met their soulmates at the wrong time have made decisions they would not have made otherwise.

- *Families have split because soulmates who met at the wrong time were unable to keep themselves from getting into an affair (if either or both were married).*

    Children must deal with the aftermath of their parent's separation after either of the parents met their soulmates at the wrong time. So, believing that your soulmate is out there and positioning yourself to meet them at the right time is a task you should undertake quickly.

- *The knowledge that timing is everything can help you maintain a positive and upbeat attitude in the face of challenges.*

    Even when you may have met your soulmate at the wrong time, knowing that time can help reposition you to experience the love of a lifetime is enough to help you hold on.

When you are about to be struck down with depressing thoughts that come from knowing that you have met your soulmate at the wrong time, remind yourself that the outcomes could have been different only if the timing was different.

You might have met them if they were not recovering from a bad relationship or going through a phase that will not allow them to be with you. With this knowledge, you can give them the time they need to recover from what is haunting them while still holding on to the faith that time can help you get together for real.

Count the cost

This applies to you the most if there are other people in the scenario except you. You may be married and have a family, and as a result, playing it by ear may not be an excellent solution for you.

There is every possibility that when you meet your soulmate, you may experience a rush of emotions that can overwhelm you. There is usually a passion between both of you, and sparks fly in all directions. The inability to handle these feelings usually results in bad decisions that affect many people in the end.

If you meet your soulmate at the wrong time in your life (especially if either of you are married), you may want to put your feet on the brakes and ask yourself a few questions, including:

- ***What is important to me right now?***

This will help you know the values you have placed in your life so far.

- *Who are the important people in my life?*

    This analysis will reveal all the people in your life who you should consider before you decide to be with someone you believe might be your soulmate.)

- *How will my decision affect them?*

    Honest answers to these questions will help you know how your actions will affect the people in your life.

    For example, it can reveal that although you may experience the thrill of something new, pursuing an affair with your soulmate who has come into your life at the wrong time may negatively affect your children in more ways than one, especially if they are still young).

When you go through this step, you will see that there may be sacrifices to be made in any case. For example, if you decide to pursue a relationship with your soulmate even when they are married; a broken home, bitter children, and a lot of persecution may result.

If, however, you decide to stay back and make things work with your spouse (if you are the married one), you may have to sacrifice that immediate pleasure for the long-term good of knowing that you were willing to stick it through till the end.

Before taking any step, please count the cost. If you think that the risk is worth it, you may go for it.

Seek professional help/guidance

This is one step you should take if you were already married or had a significant other in your life already before your soulmate came into the picture.

The decision to pull away from your marriage to be with a soulmate usually follows a season of intense marital challenges. If your soulmate steps into your life at the point where you are dealing with marital problems, there is every tendency that you will follow the promise and thrill that comes with them out of your present marriage.

However, before making this decision, you might be worthwhile to consult with a professional for help. This applies more to you if you feel that you still have a shot at salvaging your marriage or if there are already so many people in the equation (like young children).

When you and your spouse meet with a professional, they will help you in the following ways:

1. Decide if what you are feeling is worth going after.

2. Put things into perspective and count the cost associated with making such a big decision.

3. Analyze your marriage and see how you can make things work again. A professional will help you channel the emotions you are feeling towards your soulmate to your current partner, and this can be helpful if you are looking to make your marriage work, after all.

4. A professional can also help both your spouse and you through an amicable separation (if necessary).

In any case, a professional can help you navigate the boisterous season that follows meeting your soulmate at the wrong time.

Apply the brakes

This is necessary if you experience an insane level of attraction for your soulmate (especially if either of you are married). You are already getting emotional toward yourselves, and for this reason, remaining in contact may not be the best idea.

Observe the no-contact rule. The no-contact rule is that timeframe you spend away from your soulmate without trying, in any way, to contact them. During this period, you give yourself enough time to think, breathe, apply caution, and critically analyze the path you are on.

Taking time away from each other can be instrumental in getting your acts together and helping both of you make the right decisions for all the parties that will be affected if you're to continue without applying caution.

Trust the universe and allow time to work its magic

This applies when you believe there is a glimmer of hope in your situation. You may have met your soulmate when they are coming right out of a bad relationship or when they may not be in the mood for something more.

Under these circumstances, all you can do is know that time will help them heal and position them to be with you - if you really are soulmates.

However, do not entirely leave this to chance. Play your part in helping them heal (as much as they would allow you to) and take a few minutes to express to them just how genuine your feelings for them are.

You might want to make sure you let them know that you're in it for the long run, as this assurance can help them heal faster and hand your soulmate over to you.

Keep working on yourself so that timing can work in your favor

This applies the most to you if you have discovered that the things you need do not come to you when you need them. It could be an indication that you have not yet aligned yourself with the universe to get what you want at the right time.

This is not a time to despair, but a time to take the bull by the horn and get to work on yourself and your atmosphere; to make time work in your favor. There are a several things that you should make a practice of, including:

1. Start practicing the law of attraction.

The law of attraction is one of the foundational laws of the universe. In a nutshell, the law of attraction teaches that whatever you focus on and give more attention to grows.

When you apply this law in this context, it can imply that if you are constantly stressing out and you believe that you will not meet your soulmate at the right time, there is a good possibility that you may not.

To prevent this from being the case with you, begin to work on shifting your mindset from the place of stressing out over if you will meet your soulmate to the place of being convinced that you will meet them when you want to.

This way, you have a sense of being in control of your outcomes, and you will also reduce the chances of meeting your soulmate at the wrong time.

2. Position yourself to become that person to who your soulmate will be attracted to.

If you are looking to meet your soulmate and want to pursue something more with them, you should position yourself to become the kind of person your soulmate will be drawn to and who is ready to pursue something more with you.

To this end, you may need to take some time to heal from past hurts and trauma that can keep you in the same spot, even when your soulmate arrives on the scene. Also, applying the tips explained in the last chapter will help you prepare to meet your soulmate.

If you enjoyed this chapter about what to do if you meet your soulmate at the wrong time in your life, you will love the next chapter about signs that you have met your soulmate.

See you in the next chapter!

CHAPTER 5: SIGNS THAT YOU HAVE MET YOUR SOULMATE

Ignore this, and you may regret it.

So, you have spent your whole life waiting for the one. You have clung to faith, believing that against all odds, a day will come when you find the person destined to be with you.

You are not yet sure how that will happen, but one thing you know is that it must happen at the right time.

Here is the thing

You may have reached an inflection point where you have an idea of how things will pan out when you finally meet your Soulmate. All the movies you have seen and books you have read, create a picture in your mind's eye.

Your Soulmate is going to swoop in like royalty and save the day. When you finally meet this unicorn, the whole world will stop as you stare at their face and wonder how you survived all these decades without them.

But here is the challenge

While the picture I just painted may happen, no rule says it must occur the way I just described it. Several people who have met their soulmates and built enviable relationships with them did not have this experience.

If you meet these people, they will tell you stories of awkwardness that accompanied their first meeting. These stories go on to prove that there might not be a release of rose petals falling from the sky when you meet your Soulmate.

And if you ignore this fact, you may miss out on connecting deeply with your Soulmate even when you have met them.

This is what this chapter aims to help you achieve. To answer a salient question; *"how do you know that you have met your soulmate (when you eventually do)?"*

How to know that you have met your Soulmate

Here are some things that you will notice when you meet your Soulmate. These serve as indicators that you have met your Soulmate.

A. **Your Soulmate will speak your love language**

Before going any further, I need to examine the concept of *"love languages."*

A language is a medium of communication that touches your soul. It serves as a means through which one can make their intentions known to another.

Similarly, *"love languages"* are the media through which we communicate (give and prefer receiving) love. A love language demonstrates how a person expresses love to himself and another.

Generally, there are five love languages, and these include:

1. Words of affirmation

People stimulated by this love language want and value verbal communication as an expression of love. They want their partners to remind them repeatedly through words that they love them.

Telling someone you love them with passion matters most. Merely uttering the words will have no significance. People who fall into this category are pretty vocal about their need for love. When they fall in love, they do not hesitate to bear their hearts and communicate what they feel for their partners with their words.

2. Physical touch

If this is your love language, you will discover that

you feel happy when your partner does more than vocalizing their feelings for you. People with this love language value a passionate touch but non-sexual, and they do not hesitate to return the favor.

If your partner's love language (or one of them) is physical touch, they find it easy to give you a massage after a stressful day or rub your knee with one hand while they steer the car in with the other hand.

3. Service

People with this as their love language do not just want words that express how much they mean to their partners; they want to see these words in action. As Janet Jackson said in her 1986 song, *"What Have You Done For Me Lately?"*

They want their partners to convert their love for them into deeds. To these people, the smallest acts mean more than many words. The more recent the deed, the more feel your love.

If your love language is service, you will discover that you feel exhilarated when you find out that your partner handled the grocery shopping just to let you have some more time for self-care. Service in this context does not mean that you will subjugate your partner.

However, you want them to take things past the verbal *"I love you"* and perform actions that depict them in that light. Something as trivial as washing the dishes, doing the laundry, and taking the dog out for a walk makes a world of difference.

4. Quality Time

If your love language is quality time, you want your partner to consciously try to be with you if they genuinely love you.

People with this as their love language are big on having couples' hangouts, spending time together chatting, seeing movies with themselves, and so on. People of this category cherish their partners' full and undivided attention when together.

Turn off the cellphone and focus on your partner if quality time is their love language. Fiddling with your phone, returning a text, reading a book does not count as quality time just because you are in the same room together. Make your partner the number 1 focus for a few hours.

5. Receiving gifts

People who value this as their love language, love it when their partners give them gifts, no matter how trivial the gifts may seem. It could be a flower, chocolates, or just the gift of consciously trying to spend time with them.

If this is your love language, you may find yourself expecting and demanding gifts from your partner. If they cannot get you the things you require, you may slip into a mindset where you believe that they are uninterested in you and do not love you as they claim.

With these love languages explained, the first way you can know that you have met your Soulmate is that this person will speak your love language almost immediately.

Quickly, they read and understand cues that suggest your love language, and they slip into the mindset where they speak your love language. They do not see doing this as a favor to you or as a burden that they must put up with for the rest of their lives.

So, if you are at that place where you are not entirely sure whether the person in your life is your Soulmate, you may want to assess this factor. Be careful, however, not to base your decisions on this factor alone.

You must consider some factors in addition to this, and I will examine them in the next points.

B. Your life goals align

They are called your "soulmate" for a reason. This is because, amongst many other things, your Soulmate should have the same goals as you and be headed in the same direction as you. This factor is critical in your journey to finding and sticking it out with your Soulmate.

When assessing the person that you believe to be your Soulmate, there are critical questions you must ask. They include:

1. Do you both have the same goals in life; financially, professionally, and spiritually?

2. Are you both passionate about the same things; hobbies, politics, personal growth?

3. Are both of your visions aligned; 5 years from now, even 20 years down the road?

Your Soulmate should inspire you to live a life beyond where you currently breathe. This person's goals, vision, and purpose must align with yours. This is how you will help yourselves grow and become better as time progresses.

C. There's a sense of calm whenever you're around them

You should expect this one thing when you interact with that person you believe to be your Soulmate.

Your real Soulmate makes you feel at ease, and when you are with them, you know peace, calmness, and contentment like never before. All of your problems seem to melt away when your eyes make contact.

Many times, this happens as an unconscious thing. Although they may not purposefully try, they make you feel at ease when you occupy the same space. As a result, you love to be with them, and spending time in their company makes you more than just happy, but at peace with the world.

D. Your heart says yes

Let us not brush this point under the carpet because this is one of the first things experienced when you meet your Soulmate. The same way you have a deep feeling that you will get that job offer and it happens just that way is how this works.

When you meet your Soulmate, there is something about them that draws you in, and you have that assurance that they are the one for you.

When it comes to this matter, do not downplay your feelings' importance because your heart will tell you if you are with the right person. When you wake in the morning, everything about this person feels right, in alignment, and destined for success.

E. You complement yourselves

This is one of the necessary tests for knowing if they are your Soulmate. When you find your Soulmate, you discover that they perfectly match you in terms of the fact that they balance you out. Your Soulmate is a compliment for you in many areas; they complement your emotions, behaviors, and your dreams.

This is important because often, you will not be the same as your Soulmate. You both may be polar opposites in many ways, but those differences feel like something to learn from, not something to avoid. You will not have the same temperaments or behave the same.

However, in the things that matter, your Soulmate will compliment you.

For example, their cool-headed nature complements your spontaneous one or vice versa. Perhaps you love to spend money and need someone even-handed and rational to cool your excitement to spend it all but to instead save and invest.

F. You challenge yourselves

Your Soulmate challenges (not pushes) you to greatness, which brings out the best in you. A challenge is a small poke, passive-aggressive in nature. A short statement like, *"I have seen you create a better one before,"* is a little poke to do better.

The person moves to another discussion after commenting. They do not keep drilling the point, and if they do, now they are being pushy.

They challenge you to reach for your dreams and aspire you to become so much more. With your Soulmate, there is no unhealthy competition. Instead, they believe that whatever you may be doing now is only a fragment of the things you can eventually do.

As a result, they consistently challenge you to take up more significant responsibilities, smash bigger goals, and grow while you are at it. This results from the fact that your Soulmate is committed to your growth in all aspects of your life.

G. **Your Soulmate will not give you up quickly**

Let's face it. Relationships aren't usually roses and jelly beans. A time comes in every relationship that appears as though everything has gone to the depth of hell. At these points, one can either pack up and leave the relationship (which usually seems like the easy solution) or remain in the relationship and fight to preserve it.

Your relationship will not be an exception to the rule. No matter how much you love your partner, a time will come when you begin to experience these *'preserve love or die trying'* moments.

A sign that the person you are with is your Soulmate is that they will not give you up when these challenges appear. Your Soulmate possesses a history of sticking with rocky relationships instead of throwing in the towel and moving on with their lives.

When they speak about past loves, they talk about how much they tried to make wrongs right and how it pained them to walk away eventually. Your Soulmate is no fool and knows the value of their love and time.

H. The chemistry is undeniable

This is another litmus test that reveals that you have met your Soulmate. Soulmates who have connected with themselves often admit that they had chemistry, which in some cases was almost instantaneous. This matters to you if you are big on the physical stuff in your relationship.

You will most often notice that you may find it challenging to keep your hands off yourselves when you meet your Soulmate. The best part of this is that the feeling is usually not one-sided.

I. You feel secure in your relationship

When you are with your Soulmate, there's no need to feel insecure. This is because your Soulmate complements you, which implies that you are skilled in different ways. As a result, when you are with them, you feel secure.

There is usually no need to feel jealous or threatened by your Soulmate, and they make you feel safe when you are with them.

J. You feel a strong sense of empathy toward them

You are touched by what happens in the life of your Soulmate. This is not some form of distant relationship where you can go your separate ways for months on end without keeping in touch with them.

With your Soulmate, you are empathic, and the things that matter to them matter to you as well.

The connection between your Soulmate and you is one that is strong, such that whatever makes them happy makes you happy. When they experience discomfort, you are sad. When your Soulmate achieves something worthwhile, you feel it as though you were the one that championed the win.

K. You can be real with your Soulmate

Most people have a way of putting on a facade when they are with people. They feel as if they cannot be their authentic selves with people for some reason. This usually results from a fear of judgment or misunderstanding or the need to prove a point.

However, this is not the case with your Soulmate. When you are around your Soulmate, you find that you can be yourself with them. Your inner-dork emerges, and it feels good to let your dorky side shine at times.

You do not fear judgment from them. You can be entirely honest with your Soulmate and not afraid that they will judge you or make you feel stupid.

Your Soulmate is that person you can confide in without the fear of having your deepest secrets revealed to the world.

Although you may be skilled at showing people what you want them to see, your Soulmate can get you to be completely honest with them and yourself as well. You do not mind being vulnerable around your Soulmate.

L. You attach a sense of purpose to your Soulmate

Your Soulmate's entry into your life opens you up to another definition of purpose. When you meet your Soulmate, there is just this part of you that keeps reminding you that you did not only meet them because you wanted to or because you orchestrated the meeting.

Your Soulmate's entry into your world is attributed to powers beyond you. The universe and the laws of nature work as a team to place your Soulmate in random locations.

As a result, you value your relationship with your Soulmate greatly, and you would not treat them like they are just anyone else in your life.

M. Sometimes words are not needed

One of the main ingredients of a successful relationship is that there is unhindered communication between the partners. This is the same with the relationship you have with your Soulmate.

The only thing is that this time, the communication in the relationship you have with your Soulmate is much more than just words.

When you are with your Soulmate, this sense of alignment seeps into your subconscious. The more you append time with them, the more your minds become attuned to themselves. At some point, words will not be entirely necessary.

This is the point where your Soulmate understands your gestures and facial expressions and may even be able to complete your sentences for you. At this point, you begin to sound alike, and your communication happens on an even deeper level.

N. Their past relationship will not hurt the future you can have with them

Almost everyone has had their share of challenges in the past. Your Soulmate is not an exception to this. They may have had terrible relationships in the past and been through hell and hot water.

However, when they are with you, they put past negatives in the rearview mirror and allow the past to remain where it should be - in the past.

Your Soulmate will not lay the pain of past hurts at your feet. Whatever pain they experienced with past lovers does not seep into their relationship with you.

They treat you as a new beginning. Allowing you space to show your uniqueness. This is one thing that makes a relationship with your Soulmate different from the relationships you may have had in the past.

How to know if what you felt was true love

This is a topic I must do some justice to before we wrap up this chapter.

Many people have different definitions of true love. To some, true love means that the other person must be all and about them. Some people believe that their word must be law, and when they get into a relationship, they go in with this mindset.

On the other hand, some people believe that true love is all about the relationship's physical aspect. To them, their partner does not love them if they do not experience sexual penetration several days each week.

Are these true? We will find answers to this in this section of the chapter. Knowing if what you felt was true love is instrumental toward helping you understand if the relationship you are wishing will bud is worth it after all. So, here are a few signs which reveal whether what you felt was true love or not.

A. You can't bear to see the other person hurt

This is one of the first things you must consider when you are beginning to ask if you feel true love. True love cannot bear the thought of the person that it is directed toward getting hurt or dealing with pain alone.

True love is quick to take up the pain the other person feels and stops at nothing until the person it is directed at begins to heal. If what you felt was true love, you would have had this experience.

B. True love thinks long-term

When you get into a relationship with someone you feel true love for, you will discover that you think of them in the long-term. You are not just with them to kill time and have fun when bored.

You see them as part of your future, and you relate to them in that same way. As a result of this, they are a significant part of your life. You include them in all the significant decisions of your life, and you are serious about what you feel for them.

C. Their opinions matter to you

When you feel true love toward a person, you do not treat them as insignificant or as if their opinions do not matter to you. When you are about to make a decision, you think of them and what they would say about the action you want to take.

You actively seek them out and communicate your thoughts with them, after which you are vocal about wanting to hear what they have to say.

If what you feel is genuine love for them, you consider their opinions and take actions that will not hurt either of you in the end.

D. You are careful about making promises and you keep your words

Not keeping your words in a relationship is a precursor for distrust. Distrust will ultimately sever any relationship until the parties involved get tired and go their separate ways.

One way to prove that what you felt for someone is true love is that you are incredibly careful of the promises you make to them because you have a commitment that you will keep true to all the words you have said to them.

When you make a promise to someone you feel true love for, you intentionally adhere to your promise until you have accomplished what you said to them. This is because you feel strongly for them, and you do not want the distrust associated with making promises and not fulfilling them.

Being in a relationship with your Soulmate is exhilarating. It promises thrills like nothing you have ever known. Knowing what to look out for will help you identify your Soulmate when they eventually come into your life.

I dedicated this chapter to revealing signs that you have met your Soulmate. Pay attention to all fourteen signs discussed in this chapter if you do not want to experience the regret that comes with realizing that you found your Soulmate after losing them to life and chance.

The signs discussed in the last section serve as a pointer to whether what you are experiencing is true love. If, after your analysis, you discover that you are not feeling true passion for the person you are with now, this is an indication that they are not your Soulmate after all.

If you enjoyed this chapter about how to know if you have met your soulmate, you will love the next chapter about how to make love work for you.

See you in the next chapter!!

CHAPTER 6: HOW TO MAKE LOVE WORK FOR YOU

Newsflash: You must work daily for love to succeed!

So now you have met the love of your life. After waiting all these years, you have finally found the one who makes everything in your world seem brighter and the world a better place for you. You have met them, and you can tell with everything in you that the wait was worth it in the end because this person fits you perfectly.

With butterflies in your belly and the giddy feelings of happiness you have around them, you believe that it will all be a game of love and happiness forever. You do not expect that things can turn sour at some point.

One day, you argue with your soulmate, and after those heated minutes of anger, you relax on your comfortable couch with a bowl of popcorn in hand. While you mull over the activities of the last few minutes, you cannot help the shock that races through your spine.

You never believed it could happen this way

You never thought it would get to a point where you will feel so angry with your soulmate that you do not even want to see them again, at least, for a while. And that is where the problem begins.

As much as the idea of a soulmate who understands you to the latter and would not give you any trouble at all seems beautiful, it almost would not happen to you on a whim. Even after you have met your soulmate *(and you are sure that they are the one)*, your relationship with them cannot be free of hurdles and bad days.

Love works and is beautiful, but the beauty is only for those who understand this thing; fairytale love hardly ever exists. Every love story with a happy ending *(including yours)* is entirely dependent on whether the parties involved are true to themselves.

The relationship hinges on the ability to stick it out and a willingness to fight for the bond they share and know that it may take a lot of work to get the beautiful ending desired.

In a nutshell, love is not a programmable robot that works independently. Love is life, and to make it work for you, you must treat it as such; with care, the needed attention, and the determination to make it work for you.

That is what this chapter will be dedicated to; helping you make your love and relationship with your soulmate work out for the best.

What you must know if your relationship with your soulmate will be amazing

Although they are your soulmate and you feel this deep connection with them, there are things you must know to have a tremendous and blossoming relationship with them.

Over the years, many people have ignored these and thought that they are not necessary. Many others have dismissed them as old wives' tales and thought them to be of no relevance in one's relationship with their soulmate. The result of these thoughts is that although these people end up meeting their soulmates, they are unable to pursue and maintain a healthy relationship with them.

If they are unable to manage these, things that are supposed to be loving and beautiful relationships can quickly deteriorate into toxic and terrible relationships, with the two people who are supposed to be soulmates hating themselves with a fiery passion.

To avoid this from occurring, there are things you must know about your relationship with your soulmate. Pay attention to the following:

Your soulmate is human, just like you

The concept of finding your soulmate has become skewed over the last few decades, with people believing that they will find their soulmates and discover that they have hit the jackpot and found someone free of human flaws.

Well, unless you plan to date and spend the rest of your life with a ghost or an angel of sorts, this one mindset hack will help you set yourself up for a loving and beautiful relationship. The knowledge that your soulmate is human as well will do many things for you. It will help you:

1. Get rid of unnecessary and exceedingly high expectations in the relationship.

Many people crash and burn in their relationships because they have high and unbelievable expectations of the other person. Knowing that your soulmate is a human, too, will help you make room for their flaws and understand that although they may have your best interests at heart (at all times), they may fall short of your expectations from time to time.

2. Get prepared to forgive them in advance.

This point is in line with the one above. You have come to know that your soulmate will fall short of your expectations and may even hurt you sometimes *(although unintentionally)*, you can begin to prepare yourself for those times. One way to get ready is to prepare to forgive them in advance. It will not be easy, but it will be worth it in the end.

3. Become more attentive to them as well

When you realize that your soulmate is human, you become more conscious of them than you would have if you were to treat them like an apparition that fell out of the sky or a robot sent by the universe to satisfy your every whim.

The knowledge that your soulmate is a person as you are will help you remember that they have emotions just like you. Some things irritate, excite, annoy, or make your partner happy. Armed with this knowledge, you can look out for the things they like and play your part in making them happy for as long as your relationship lasts.

4. Challenges will come up as you journey towards building the life of your dreams

As much as this is one thing that many people run away from, failure to confront it head-on does not change the fact that it is the truth and nothing short of that.

As you get on with building an enviable relationship with your soulmate, be aware that a time will come when things will not be as rosy as you may have expected. You may experience a rough patch along the way.

If you cannot conceive these ideas in your mind as you get into a relationship and have a contingency plan in place ready, you may give up at the first sign of resistance.

5. *You must be committed to getting to 'happily-ever-after'*

Well, that is if you want your relationship with your soulmate to end up in a 'happily-ever-after' state.

The 'happily-ever-after' state is one thing that many love stories have been able to document and display over time; the hurdles those in love must go through to get a shot at the lives they want in the end. Borrow a leaf from these stories even as you venture into a relationship with your soulmate.

As much as you may not want to hear this, life may not let you have your soulmate and experience a happily-ever-after without throwing you some curveballs. The universe will test you before you can have whatever you desire. One of those tests you will have to pass in your relationship with your soulmate is the ability to stick it through till the end. One easy way to achieve this is by making a list of all the worst-case scenarios.

What are the things that can go wrong in your relationship with your soulmate? Brainstorm these possible situations and begin to create a way to weather them together.

The idea is not to bail at the sight of the slightest challenges but to be the soulmate who will stick close and help them through their darkest times.

What you need to make love work for you

Making love work for you is something you should have at the top of your mind right now. This is because you will only truly be happy when you have found your soulmate, proven to the universe that you are meant to be together, and you get to start building the 'happily-ever-after' of your dreams.

However, to make love work for you, there are some skills that you must possess. Skills are not only needed when you are looking to start a new job or establish a new business to get the bucks rolling in.

To have an enviable relationship with your soulmate, you need a plethora of soft skills. This section takes a quick look at these skills and where they are necessary for your relationship.

1. Communication

Communication is more than the lifeblood of every relationship, and your relationship with your soulmate is not exempted from this. Suppose communication is absent or stilted in your relationship.

In that case, it is only a matter of time before your relationship hits an iceberg and is submerged under the boisterous water called life.

The function of communication in any relationship cannot be overemphasized. Here's why communication is necessary for your relationship.

A. Communication helps you establish a connection with your soulmate in a way nothing else can.

This is because when you communicate *(verbally and non-verbally)* with your partner, you open yourself up to them and allow them to know what is happening with you in real-time.

This way, your soulmate can help you when you desperately need it and can also be there when you need someone to be happy with.

This one key will strengthen your relationship tremendously; the ability to communicate effectively.

B. *Communication helps you make the best decisions in your relationship.*

When your soulmate is transparent with you about the things they like or do not like, you can experience them in a way that they love. This way, you do not set them off or trigger unfavorable responses in them toward you. The same thing happens when you return the favor.

C. *Communication eliminates suspicion and distrust in any relationship.*

When distrust, suspicion, and paranoia begin to seep into a relationship, a partner starts to feel like the other is withholding something. The danger with this is that when it happens, there is every tendency that the other person's mind can take advantage of the darkness it is in to create ambiguous pictures and make a molehill appear as though it is a mountain.

The result is that if left unattended, the relationship can hit the rocks at any time as the people in the relationship begin to feel estranged from themselves. This can happen to you even if you are in a relationship with your soulmate.

To prevent this from taking place, make it a point of duty to communicate effectively with them. Are they having a bad day? Talk to your soulmate.

Are they feeling frustrated about something or someone? Hear them out without offering solutions. You do not always need to fix a problem; try to absorb the feelings of the person experiencing the pain. Even if there's good stuff happening around you, tell them.

For the sake of your relationship's health, never leave your soulmate in the dark. Also, in the spirit of communicating, carving out time to spend with them and giving them your full attention is also a form of communication.

2. Remembering the small things

While this may be subjective and depends on your interpretation of what matters to you and what does not, remembering the small things in any relationship is one skill that can make all the difference.

Something as little as remembering that your soulmate loves their coffee with a bit of cream in it, or the day they got their first contract and celebrating it with them, can show them that they are essential to you.

This has a way of going beyond the usual *"I love you"* and *"You are special to me"* chant that everyone seems to drop on their partner sooner or later. It reiterates the fact that if you can remember the tiny things about them *(especially the things that matter to them, like their favorite color or best meal),* it means that you pay attention to them.

Remembering the small things in your relationship is one way to tell your soulmate that they are essential to you, deserve your undivided attention, and that you are not afraid to make them feel special any chance you get.

3. **Knowing the magic words and when to use them.**

We established in an earlier section that relationships will not always be easy. Notwithstanding how much you try to, there will always be those times when you may have differences with your partner. These are the times when this skill is needed.

For a relationship to work, both parties must make it a point of duty to know when to get off their high horses and allow themselves to be vulnerable for the long-term safety of their relationship. Pride and healthy relationships have never been two peas in a pod and never will be.

And an expression of satisfaction is the inability to identify and effectively use the magic words; *"sorry," "thank you,"* and *"please."* As small as these words seem, they play a significant role in any successful relationship. Here's how they work.

A. "Sorry": A perfect way to use this is in the sentence "I am sorry." It shows that you know that something has happened in a way that it should not have. You are taking responsibility for it, and you are willing to do better. This is one way to get your soulmate to forgive you even when you make the mistakes you are bound to make in the relationship. Many relationships have gone south because neither person understood this nor did their best to follow through.

Apologizing can take a lot of courage. It suggests that you understand that you have made a mistake, and doing it requires that you get off your high horse.

However, the dividends of knowing when you are wrong and taking the responsibility of apologizing to your partner are immense. Imbibing this character is one way to make sure that your relationship lasts an exceedingly long time.

B. "Thank you": Using this phrase implies that you are appreciative of a kind gesture and that you do not see it as something you had the right to.

Thank you is a sure sign that you are not battling with an entitlement mentality. It is an acknowledgment of the efforts of your soulmate in your relationship.

To build a healthy relationship with your soulmate, you must express appreciation for any and everything - no matter how small it might appear. Vocalizing your appreciation by the proper use of the words "thank you" can go a long way to help you maintain a healthy and happy relationship.

C. "Please": This is also another word that shows that you aren't battling with the entitlement mindset. Many people do not use this word often, and it is a reflection that they think/believe that their wishes should be their partners' commands. If you do not make it a point of duty to communicate to your partner that you are soulmates *(and you do not intend to use them as some form of cheap help)*, you may want to incorporate this word into your vocabulary for everyday use.

4. **Understand your partner**

We established in an earlier section of this chapter that although you are getting into a relationship with your soulmate, you must consciously remember that they are humans as well.

In line with that, when you have come to terms with the fact that you are in a relationship with a person that you love, it is your job to understand them. Look out for these points if you want to have a successful relationship.

A. Understand their personality/temperaments.

Your soulmate's temperament is a significant part of your relationship, and understanding it is vital. Since your partner's temperament is a huge part of their entire personality, you may want to spend time to figure it out.

When you have understood their temperament/personality, you can figure out how you complement yourselves.

B. Understand their boundaries

All of us have those lines we have created in our lives; invisible lines that no one can cross. To keep enjoying your soulmate, you may want to take out time to understand their boundaries.

What things make them tick and get them emotionally excited? What are the things that they love, hate, and most of all, the things that they find revulsive?

When you have answered these questions, you can make better decisions that concern them and position yourself to be the partner they want to be in a long-term relationship with.

C. Their love language

In an earlier chapter, we discussed the five love

languages. As you journey toward building an enviable relationship with your soulmate, you must understand their primary love language.

This knowledge will help you communicate your love for them in a way that they can easily understand, interpret, and cherish.

Trying to express love by giving only gifts to someone whose primary love language is 'words of affirmation' may not carry the same weight as it would if you are to say the magic words to them again.

5. Consciously work on your love until it grows to become something sustainable

Love is more than the emotions and fluttery feelings that come with finding your soulmate the first time. If you are to grow your relationship into something worthwhile and stand the test of time, your love and feelings must become sustainable.

The question in your head is, "*how do you achieve this?*" Allow me to give you a few pointers.

A. Pay attention to making sure that your needs are met

And by *"your,"* what is meant is the both of you. You must pay attention to your soulmate and ensure that you meet their needs on all levels;

physically, emotionally, mentally, and in all areas.

They must also commit to doing the same thing for you. As your relationship progresses, your soulmate must become the person to whom you run to when you have a challenge and need help.

When you begin always to seek the support and attention of someone who is not your soulmate, it may be a sign that your relationship may already be in some trouble.

B. Focus on respect and make sure this goes both ways.

For any relationship to flourish, both parties must be intentional about mutual respect. It is practically impossible for a relationship to last for a long time if one party makes it a point of duty to be at the receiving end of all the love, attention, and respect without giving back.

We have established the fact that your soulmate is a human as well. The way you want to be respected is the same way you should make it a point of duty to return the favor to your soulmate. When the relationship has both of you respecting yourselves and each other's ideologies about life, it will last for much longer.

C. Do not be ashamed to be vulnerable with your soulmate

Although you may project yourself as a strong person who cannot be moved by anything, this should not be your focus in your relationship with your soulmate. When you seek to get to your *'happily-ever-after,'* you must make it a point of duty to consciously make yourself vulnerable to them.

Let them see the real you that you do not show the rest of the world. This will help inspire confidence and trust in you, even as they do the same for you.

D. Establish passionate communication

This goes beyond having shallow conversations with your soulmate. Passionate communication is vital to secure your relationship and ensure that you end up in the *'happily-ever-after'* you seek.

You must feel something during, and after each time you communicate with your partner, they must also feel that energy. If you or your partner feel nothing powerful after 'communicating,' then you never truly communicated; you both merely spoke to each other.

Train yourself to confide in your soulmate. They need to be aware of all the details of your life if they are to stick with you and be with you in the relationship for the long haul. Communication is vital to ensure that doubts and suspicions do not take root and destroy your relationship as it unfolds.

The benefits of communication in a relationship have been outlined in an earlier section of this chapter. Do well to refer to that section when you feel that keeping your soulmate in the loop is unnecessary.

While it feels great to be in a relationship with your soulmate, you must know that it will not work without effort. If your love will go the way you want and lead to a happy ending, you must be willing to give it your best shot. Pay attention to the tips discussed in this chapter and watch your love stay secure and grow.

If you enjoyed this chapter about how to make love work in your relationship, I just know you're going to love the next chapter about how sex plays a role in keeping your soulmate.

See you in the next chapter!

CHAPTER 7: HOW SEX PLAYS A ROLE IN KEEPING YOUR SOULMATE

Ignore sex at your own peril

SEX; one of the most controversial and misunderstood words in relationships. Many feelings are elicited in many people's minds at the mention of this word. For some people, sex is that thing that should not be talked about, heard about, or even thought of until one is married.

These people believe that parents should not even have the *"sex"* conversation with their adolescent children because they would be corrupting them or feeding them the wrong information.

For the people in this category, if someone thinks of sex without being in a marriage, they believe that person has some sort of moral challenge.

Sitting pretty at the other side of the pendulum are people who believe that *"sex"* is terrific. From the time these people hit adolescence and figured out what their sexual organs were for, they began a never-ending journey of exploration; chasing down sexual fantasies and living in the moment.

For people in this category, life is nothing without a bit of fun and the thrill of intense pleasure that comes with having sexual contact with another person. When they eventually get into a romantic relationship, they quickly assess their partner's sexual prowess. If their partner is not up to par, they may have to call the relationship quits.

When it comes to sex, you must understand that it is a significant part of any relationship. Especially if you want your relationship to last for a long time and lead to a *'happily-ever-after.'* This is because of the significance of sex and the bond it creates in people's lives in a relationship.

In any case, we will look at the subject of *"sex"* and evaluate the role it must play in your relationship with your soulmate if you want a relationship that never ends.

What is 'SEX?'

It seems like a silly question to ask. When we talk about 'sex,' we're not referring to the gender you were born as or the one you identify with at the moment. Sex in this context is the verb, the physical act of joining as one with your soulmate.

Wikipedia defines *'sex'* with the phrase; *"human sexual activity/ human sexual practice."*

According to Wikipedia, this is how humans express and experience a spiritual awakening. *"Spiritual"* not in the religious sense, but in a total *"out-of-body"* experience, almost like a drug high.

As a matter of fact, sex is a broad term that encompasses a multitude of actions aimed at giving those involved in the act *(yourself and your soulmate, in this context)* an avenue to express themselves and experience the feelings, passion, attraction, and lust of the other person.

This action dates back to the beginning of time, and the need to have physical contact with another person is a thirst that everyone is bound to experience in their lives at some point.

What you need to know about sex

Before we get on with the subject, there are some records we must set straight. These are the mainstream ideas that may hold you back and prevent you from having a fulfilling sexual experience, even when you are with your soulmate. Please note these points that I discuss in this section before proceeding and completing this chapter.

1. It is difficult to define the right/wrong way to have sex

This is one thing you need to know about the subject of sex; there is no one-size-fits-all approach to it. Although this may sound a bit far-fetched to you, there are different strokes for different folks in this context, literally.

If you must have a satisfying sexual life with your soulmate, you must understand that some of the things that make you tick will not set off their alarms at all. There are about a thousand different sexual activities, and you may discover that your soulmate has a preference for sexual activity you may not have heard of before.

What this also implies is that you may not be abnormal as you may think you are. Many people are held back from exploring the boundaries of their sexual lives with their soulmates simply because they have sexual urges that they believe are unhealthy or unheard of. This may not be true.

Since it is difficult to define a right/wrong approach to sex, you must consciously set a boundary to it. As is the case with every healthy thing, you must understand what you accept or otherwise do not. While doing this, pay attention and make sure that what you believe is fun for you does not hurt the other person involved.

Sex is about pleasure and an avenue to express your love for your soulmate. It should not be used as an outlet or a way to inflict pain on your partner or, vice versa, to deal with stress in your life.

2. To enjoy sex, you must be comfortable

This is one thing that not many people today possess: comfort. In today's world, comfort looks like a far-fetched topic. Here is what is meant by comfort.

Comfort, in this context, is the feeling of satisfaction that comes from knowing that you are human and unforgettable just the way you are. Although many people today walk around in the best of clothes and look satisfied with themselves, a good number of them are not comfortable. This discomfort is the result of several reasons, including:

A. Unhealthy comparisons

This is usually the result of an internalized action, generally known as *"body shaming."* Body Shaming is the practice of making a mockery of someone by criticizing or making them feel horrible about their body size or shape. Body shaming can be internal *(happening within the person)* or external *(coming from other people)*.

When people are compared or compare themselves against others like the picture-perfect models they see in movies or music videos or just someone they would rather look like, the result is that over time, they begin to look down on their bodies. Under these conditions, they start believing that they are not attractive. Any compliment about their body shape will be taken as a form of criticism.

A person who struggles with body-shaming is not likely to enjoy sex with their partner. Because they are already cynical toward themselves, they are unwilling to take compliments *(even in the heat of the physical activity)*. They will most likely not loosen up enough to enjoy intimacy with their partner.

B. The idea that they are 'weird'

When someone harbors the notion that they are weird or strange for some reason (especially regarding their sexuality and sexual preferences), there is every tendency that they will be unable to loosen up enough and enjoy sex with their partner.

Sometimes, this idea of weirdness comes when the person discovers that they like something that is not mainstream, that they have some strange fetish, and they may not know that there exist other people just like themselves.

The way around this is to start by exposing yourself to the world. Take some time to get out of your head. To achieve this, you may want to talk to an expert on sexual health or a psychologist who can help you break down what you feel and show you how you may want to go about it to get the best results.

3. An active sex life can prove to be a vital part of your relationship

While this may be a subjective statement, it still holds true. Some people may not agree that sex is vital except when married to your soulmate.

Others may see sex as a non-negotiable factor in the relationship. In any case, sex is essential, and that is what we will spend the rest of this chapter discusses.

For the best results, you may want to spend some time talking to your soulmate about what they believe and hold as true when it comes to sex. This is the only way to make sure that both of you are on the same page regarding sex.

4. For sex to work, you must be compatible with your partner

This is related to the first point I made in this section of the program; different people have different sexual preferences.

Pay attention to your partner and be sure to understand their sexual preferences. This way, you can know what they want and how you can meet their sexual needs.

Why do people have sex?

Now that we have cleared the air and established a few things you need to know about sex, we must examine why people have sex. When we have explained these, you will begin to understand why you feel the urge to have sex with your soulmate *(or maybe not)*.

1. Sex is an expression of deep emotions

As hinted in the definition of sex, one of the primary reasons people have sex is that sex is a channel through which they can express their feelings to their soulmate, especially when they want this to go beyond words.

This goes beyond the mindless activity of having a quick romp in the sack with another random person.

Under these conditions *(when they want to express their feelings for their soulmate)*, they refer to it as *"making love."*

This phrase implies that they are doing more than the physical activity. To them, it is about the emotional and psychological connection that accompanies having sex *(or making love)*.

2. To achieve a desired aim

Although this may sound obvious, many people have sex to achieve a desired aim. When the objective is met, there is little or no commitment from either party. Some of these goals may include having a baby, improve a person's social standing *(move from low status in a group to become much more popular)*, or exerting revenge in some cases.

3. Pressure

This is the side of sex that is not pleasing at all. Sometimes, people have sex because of the pressure they come under.

This pressure could be from friends *(to conquer the fear of missing out or feel like they belong)* or the pressure from a partner *(which they may give in to so that they can stop being pestered or as a way of preventing something terrible from happening like the exit of that partner from a relationship)*.

Notwithstanding what form it takes, having sex because of being placed under undue pressure is not healthy for you. As much as it lies within you, walk away from any person or situation where you are pressured to have sex, especially when you feel like you are not yet ready for it.

4. Sexual curiosity

Some people do not begin their sexual journey with the assuredness of who they really are or what they want sexually from their partner. This leads to confusion when they meet someone that they feel attraction for.

These people are usually curious and have many things on their minds.

As a result of the confusion they experience, they may begin to try out many things sexually. This confusion leads to their having sex because of curiosity. Sometimes, they may find the answers they seek. Sometimes, they may not.

Why is sex important in maintaining relationships?

Let's deep-dive into several reasons why sex is essential in relationships.

1. The emotional connection that comes with it

In the previous section, we established that sex is important because it provides people with a channel to express their emotions. This is one of the first reasons why sex is essential in your relationship with your soulmate.

If you are looking to transform the words "I love you" to a new form of expression where your soulmate begins to trust and believe it for real, you may want to try adding sex to your relationship.

Under these conditions, you must not approach sex as an activity you are compelled to engage in. Instead, you must work hard to make it a memorable experience for your partner and make sure that you can communicate your emotions' depths with them.

2. **A healthy sex life can help you/your partner build self-esteem**

Remember how we discussed body shaming and how it can threaten a person's sexual life? A healthy sex life with your partner can serve to help you regain your self-esteem *(if you have lost it at some point)* or vice versa *(if your partner is the one affected).*

During the act, your partner's love, attention, and adoration are channeled toward you while you do the same thing for them. Being in the center, love and attention can be pivotal toward helping you regain your sense of self-esteem.

As your partner tells you how beautiful you are to them, these words and reassurance can override the effects of every bad word and thought you might have harbored about yourself in years past.

As you allow this action to go on and continue over time, your partner's assertions and emotions start getting registered in your subconscious, and this is what accounts for the surge in self-esteem that you will notice.

For this to work, your partner needs to be lavish with attention and care even while they make love to you. If your partner also needs a self-esteem boost, you must be conscious about returning the favor.

3. The reproductive factor

This is one of the foremost reasons why people have sex; for the sake of reproduction. If you are married to your soulmate, or you are not opposed to the idea of having children, you may want to get physically involved with your partner so that the both of you can make children while at it.

4. Stress relief

Research shows that sex is a great way to eliminate stress and tension when these weigh down on you. This is yet another reason why sex must be a part of your relationship with your soulmate.

If you are the kind that gets stressed all the time *(or your partner is)*, there is every tendency that they would love to relate to you sexually. Allowing yourself to get involved in the act can afford you the opportunity to help your soulmate get rid of stress while they return the favor to you as well.

5. Health benefits

Surprisingly, there are many health benefits associated with a healthy sex life. Some of them include:

A. Sex can be a mild form of exercise.

This should not be shocking because there is a reason why you work up a sweat when you have had sex. A survey carried out corroborated this theory. So, you may want to add that to the pool of reasons why you would incorporate sex into your list of activities to be done with your soulmate.

B. People with a healthy sex life are generally healthier than those who do not have this.

The immune systems of people with a good sex life seem to perform better, and they are known to be stronger, maintaining a healthy balance in life. They get sick less often and recover from illness faster.

C. Improved memory.

A study was carried out which showed that people between the ages of 50-90, who have a healthy sex life, are more likely to have better memories than their age mates who do not have positive sex lives.

When all these health benefits are looked at, you can safely say that with healthy sex in your relationship, there are more reasons for you and your partner to enjoy the relationship and stay together longer, if not forever.

6. **A healthy sex life strengthens your relationship beyond the four walls of your bedroom**

When it comes to your sex life, the rewards you get when you have a healthy one goes beyond the four walls of your bedroom. It is easy to identify people who have been intimate with each other, even when you see them outside the bedroom. For these people, there is an affection and ease that they feel around one another.

If your love language is personal touch, you may find the ease that comes with being intimate with your soulmate as an incentive for them to be cozy with you and not ashamed to express their love for you even in public.

However, for the sake of decency, you may want to keep things appropriate for all audiences when you are in public.

7. After great sex comes a good night's sleep

If you or your partner battles insomnia, you may want to pay more attention to this point. Research and patterns have shown that after great sex, the body's natural response falls into a state of deep sleep. So, here's how it works:

At the climax of sexual activity, your body releases an enzyme known as Prolactin. Among many things that "prolactin" does, it can lead to deeper and more relaxed sleep and more intriguing dreams *(better sleep in the REM phase)*.

This is why once you orgasm; your body's next response is to fall into a state of satisfaction, and if you aren't careful to prevent it from happening, you will discover that your eyes will begin to slip shut.

How to be a better lover for your lover

It is not enough to understand what sex is and why it is vital in your relationship. You must know how to make yourself a better lover for your soulmate.

That was the whole idea behind this chapter; to equip you with the knowledge you need to become a better lover. To become better with your lover, here are a few things you must do:

1. **Normalize being vulnerable with them**

This is one of the basic requirements for having sex with your soulmate. If you are to enjoy the activity, you must allow yourself to become vulnerable with them and let go of control at some point. Sex is all about trust, and to trust someone, you must allow yourself to become vulnerable.

2. **Listen to them as well**

We are talking about a relationship here, not a one-sided case of infatuation and misguided emotions. To make the most of your sexual life with your soulmate/partner, understand that it is not all about you.

They have needs just like you do, and listening to them not only makes them feel appreciated, but it also instructs you to know what you must do to make your sex life better.

3. **Be intentional about showing your soulmate love and respect as you make love to them**

Especially if you know that they either suffer from body shaming or battle with low self-esteem. The psychology behind this has been explained in-depth in earlier sections of this chapter.

Be sure to add this to your bucket list of activities because once your partner builds their self-esteem, it will show during sex. They may have the audacity to try out new stuff with you, thereby spicing up your sex life.

4. **Teach yourself to speak their love language**

Above and beyond the physical activity, you seek an experience with your soulmate. An experience of intimacy and oneness with them. To achieve this, you need much more than sex. You must know how to make your partner feel loved and appreciated when they are with you.

One way to do this is by teaching yourself how to speak your partners' love language. When you begin to express their love language, you will notice that they get more attuned to you like a blooming flower.

As this happens, rest assured that you are getting them to trust you, and this will make the lovemaking experience with them much better as time moves forward.

How to get your lover to be better for you

Just as we established earlier, it is a two-way street. Apply the following strategies to get your lover to be a better lover for you:

1. **Talk to them**

Your soulmate is not some ghost with superpowers of knowing everything. Do not assume that your soulmate knows what you like and what you do not with respect to your sexual life and preferences. It is your duty to educate them and do this as many times as needed.

2. **Be ready to compromise**

Since you are striving to build an enviable future with your soulmate, one way to win this war can be to put down your verbal-gun at some point and decide to call a truce.

In this context, this means connecting with your soulmate *(by practicing step one above)* and deciding on how to do things so that everyone benefits in the end.

They may not be able to meet all of your sexual needs, but the idea is that they get to a point where they meet most of your needs.

Healthy compromise is one way to do this. Sex is a significant part of most healthy relationships. If you chose to allow it to be a part of your relationship, it is imperative that you do it properly by using the tips and strategies discussed in this chapter.

As you just learned, sex can play a positive role in your relationship, but finding your soulmate does not guarantee that your relationship will last forever. In the next chapter, I explain to you why.

See you in the next chapter!

CHAPTER 8: WHY FINDING YOUR SOULMATE DOES NOT GUARANTEE THE RELATIONSHIP WILL LAST LONG

Nothing in life is guaranteed, especially love!

You may have harbored ideas peddled by romance movies and sappy books. These ideas usually show that once soulmates have found themselves, they fight through many challenges and stroll into a happily-ever-after.

While this happens at times, you must face reality here; and the truth is that this is not always the case. Even after meeting your soulmate, there is no guarantee that you will be together for the rest of your lives. For one, they may be married or tethered to someone else (and happily so).

They may not be seeking anything more from you than friendship, or something else may stop you from getting the happy ending you desire with your soulmate.

In any case, things may not work out, even after you have found your soulmate. This chapter will examine this uncommon truth and see why this happens to some people and steps you can take to reduce it from happening to you.

So you think that you have found your soulmate?

This program's whole point is to open your eyes to what you must do to find your soulmate and offer guidance on what you must do when you have found them.

However, you may be at a point where you try to make things work with a person you believe is your soulmate. If you take a step back and discover that you are doing your best to make things work with them and things are not, you may want to ask yourself a critical question. Are they indeed the one?

Asking and answering this question can be instrumental as it will open your eyes to see if you are walking the right path or wasting your time and resources on a person you should not be.

No matter how far you think you have traveled down the relationship road, you must look out for red flags that show you are with the wrong person.

You cannot make things work with the wrong

person, no matter how hard you try. Here are a few red flags; signs that the person you think is your soulmate is not who you think they are.

1. You both want different things

Remember how we discussed that with your soulmate, you should know that you both want the same things? This is not the case with a person who is not your soulmate. Even if you look at them and feel the chemistry, this is one factor you must consider carefully before committing to anything with anyone.

Your *"non-soulmate"* will be on a different journey, and most times, you will discover that what you want and what they want are two opposite ends that should never meet.

In line with this, your values will be different, and your attitude towards life will be dissimilar. Priorities will not be complementary, and in general, the both of you will be like the North and South poles *(too distant to interact with yourselves)*.

The result of this is that your relationship will be fraught with differences, and challenges will keep coming up as you go. A clear example is that you may want to have a large family while they may not want kids at all. This one thing can create a massive gap between the both of you and drive the relationship into the ground.

2. They won't return your gesture of honesty and openness

Honesty is a critical part of every successful relationship, and although you will be interested in making things work, they will not be too eager to return the gesture.

You will discover that there is a lot of secrecy and hiding with this person. They will be more likely to trust other people, except you, and find it hard to have conversations where they will need to be vulnerable with you.

3. They will give you hints

We often get hints that a person should not be there in our lives. They may not say it with their mouths, but their actions and everything in between will tell you that they are not the one for you.

You will notice that all your love and attention is one-sided, and when you try to confront them, they may come clean with you and tell you that you are not the one for them.

As much as this pulling away may be one of the most challenging things for you to do, your best line of action will be to pull the plug on the relationship. Walk away because you deserve better.

4. **They abuse you**

Abusing you is one red flag you cannot afford to turn blind eyes to. Your soulmate understands the value of your sanity and will do nothing to compromise it. On the other hand, when you are with someone who is not your soulmate and who has little or no affection for you, they do not see abusing you as a big deal.

Abuse comes in many forms, and you do not have to wait until the person hits you or does anything to harm your body for you to see the signs before you. The wrong person may subject you to other forms of abuse that are not physical but mental and emotional in nature.

They do this to exercise control over you and get you under their grip. This is the bottom line of abuse, and making excuses for them will not change the fact that you need to confront the facts before you immediately.

5. **They aren't there for you**

There are times when you need the attention of your soulmate, but they may be unable to rise to the occasion. This can be understandable and utterly different from what we discuss in this section.

The wrong person is never there for you when you need them. Usually, this happens more than once. Since both of you will most likely have different interests, there is every tendency that they will never be able to support you.

For any relationship to work, support is crucial, and this must come from both sides of the relationship. When your partner makes it a point of duty to let you handle everything in your life all by yourself *(physically, mentally, emotionally, and in every dimension)*, this may be a sign that you are with the wrong person.

6. **They talk down on your vision**

Your soulmate should be your biggest cheerleader. However, when you discover that the person you want to make things work with is continuously in the business of making you feel stupid for having big dreams, take that as a sign of something more serious.

As a result, your self-esteem may be harmed. You may get to a point where it feels as though you cannot achieve a lot, and you may lose the zeal to be optimistic about life while still pursuing your ambitions. Being with the wrong person does more to you than just physically hurting you.

Why soulmate relationships do not always work out

As much as this may not be the most effortless conversation for you, finding your soulmate is not always a guarantee that the relationship will work out.

If the person you are with does not tick the points communicated in the last section, you want to consider the next few issues. These are reasons why soulmates do not always end up together.

1. **When you meet your soulmate at the wrong time of life**

In an earlier chapter, we explored the concept of the wrong time in detail. The truth is, if you meet your soulmate at this time, you will have to fight through a lot to make things work. However, if they are not interested in fighting for you as well, the relationship may not blossom.

For example, suppose you meet your soulmate and discover that they are happily married to someone else and are in no way looking to get out of the marriage. In that case, there is every tendency that your relationship with them will not lead to a happily-ever-after.

Another classic example of this is if you meet your soulmate at a time when they are straight out of a bad relationship, still hurting deeply, and in no place to look for anything more. Your relationship with them will be negatively affected.

2. **Demands from society and loved ones**

Although this sounds like something from the 1800s, some parents still forbid their children from marrying or dating someone of a different racial or ethnic background. This can prove challenging as you look to build a life with your soulmate after finding them.

Although they may love you, this person may feel a deep sense of indebtedness to their parents and may not want to go against them.

Religion can pose a substantial barrier to being with your soulmate. Some religions believe and teach that it is a sin and wrong for a person who is part of them to marry someone from another religious background.

This forms a significant block when building a life with your soulmate. Although they might love you, they need the blessings and approval of their family and religious leader to pursue a long-term commitment with you.

There is also the challenge of societal views on specific subjects. The issue of a person's sexuality and gender identification can threaten you if you are looking to build a life with them. For example, if a man found out that his soulmate is of the same gender, pursuing a relationship with him may be challenging or downright impossible *(depending on the societal context in question).*

The result is that many people have been pushed to the point where they have to let go of their soulmate or began to live lives of secrecy while still living up to the demands that society, family, or religious groups have placed on them.

3. **Personal challenges**

Some soulmate relationships end up not

blossoming because one or both partners may be dealing with acute personal problems. One partner may not be inclined towards being on the receiving end of such issues for long.

For example, it's not easy to deal with a soulmate that overanalyzes everything *(every gesture and conversation)*, is cynical and does not trust you. This alone can be a dealbreaker on different levels.

4. **Unrealistic expectations**

If you do not make it a point of duty to correct this immediately, you may fall into this trap. Your soulmate is a person that is meant for you. You feel a deep connection between both of you, and sometimes this may even be on a spiritual level. This does not negate the fact that your soulmate is human and that there is only so much they can do for you.

Unrealistic expectations can kill your relationship and make a quick mess of it; that is if you let it consume you. Yes, there are things your soulmate must-do for you. Do not make it a point of duty to believe that they will be there for you at every turn.

Unrealistic expectations, like the belief that your soulmate relationship will be nothing short of beautiful, will only cause you untold heartache. If not careful, you might throw this relationship away simply because you got your hopes too far up in the sky.

Your soulmate is human and having unrealistic expectations will place them under undue pressure. As time proceeds, this can cause your relationship to fail.

5. **People change**

This is one thing you must know if you will be successful with your relationship. Although they may be the one for you presently, people change in the future. You and your partner may become very different people 2, 5 or even 20 years from today.

At the beginning of your journey, they may want you; craving your love, attention, and all that. However, you may notice a few drastic changes as time unfolds. The passage of time may reveal that they are changing, just like everything in life does. Many people ask the million-dollar question: *"Why has my partner changed?"* To proceed, we must answer this question in-depth.

Here are a few reasons why people change.

A. Growth

Personal growth is a significant and foundational reason why people change. When you grow, you discover a different approach to life, a new set of values, new priorities, and many things about you become new.

Take this as an example: When you were a child, some games were the highlight of your life. You lived for them, looked forward to them, and spent your free time playing these games.

When you became a teenager, these games changed meaning for you. As you grew into adulthood, you shed them entirely and moved on to grapple with the challenges of adulthood. It happens the same way with your soulmate.

When they begin to grow *(in age and other dimensions of life),* there is every tendency that you will notice new things about them. They may stop being the people you knew, adopt new lifestyles, and these may affect your relationship; either positively or negatively.

Growth will change your soulmate in more ways than you expected, especially as they begin to grapple with more responsibilities.

B. Exposure that increases options

Exposure is an important point we must discuss in this chapter. *Exposure (or options)* comes with a change in the way people see things and how they interact with life. Exposure widens a person's options.

Consider this scenario: You met your soulmate as a college student. Both of you happen to be college classmates. It is love at first sight, and you can almost vow that you will be together forever.

That is great until both of you are done with college and you move to different parts of the country to get established and seek opportunities that can help you become all you want in life. In the new place, you meet a new person, and they catch your fancy in ways you never expected.

You feel connected with this new person, although you promised yourself you would not. As much as you try to turn blind eyes to it, you cannot rule out the fact that there is something about this new person that draws you in. What do you think will happen when after a period of being with this new person?

Do you think that you will have the same enthusiasm to see your sweetheart from college again? Do you think things will automatically revert to the way they were before?

One thing happened to you - exposure. Your options increased, and you started questioning what you knew before. This can happen to your soulmate when exposed to more options.

Exposure is a significant factor responsible for drastic changes in people. They may have met someone else and now believe that you are not their soulmate after all. The way to make sure that you are not making a mistake is by giving yourself more options.

Even when you have found the one you believe is your soulmate, you may want to take some time to explore more options before making a lasting commitment. Meet more people, travel, and have fun. The same applies to your soulmate.

C. People get bored

At the beginning of your relationship, you were excited. The novelty of all that you felt for them excited you in no small way. The same could be said for them until this relationship started getting older.

Suddenly, your soulmate began to change how they relate to you. This may result from getting tired of the relationship or the lack of thrill in it.

Humans are excitement freaks. We enjoy the thrill of something new. That is why it is easier to start a new business than to grow an existing one. When your soulmate gets tired of the relationship, they may begin to act flippant, dismissive of you, eager to spend more time away from you. They may get apathetic toward everything that has to do with the relationship.

At this point, the spark dies down. The chemistry you felt at the beginning can almost be thought of as a thing of the past. To salvage the relationship, you need to seek ways to bring back the relationship's spice. All your activities at this point should point toward rekindling the flame of your passion - the one you felt at the beginning.

If you do not do this, you run the risk of losing your soulmate to the next available person as your partner searches for excitement.

How can these changes affect your relationship, and what you can do about them

Changes in attitude and character can affect your relationship in many ways. Some of them include:

1. Your partner begins to see you in ways they did not before.

In this context, this is a bad way. You no longer look sexy enough for them, and their interest in continuing the relationship drops. You may want to spend some time talking with them.

This is one case where complete honesty and openness are needed in a relationship. Listen to them and hear what it is about you that they are less excited about and the things they would rather that you start doing. With this knowledge, you can tweak things and improve your relationship.

2. When the trigger for this change is

exposure (other options), you will notice that someone else becomes the center of your partner's world.

They would rather spend more time with that person than with you. They may start keeping secrets and acting suspiciously when you are around.

If your partner got exposed to someone else and decide that this new person is better for them after all, it is best to grant them their wish. Take a bow and let them go. This will not be easy; especially if you have come to love and cherish them. Realize that you have options too. In a previous chapter, I gave you many ways to meet your soulmate. You may need to dust off that chapter and use it again.

You should never need to beg anyone to be with you. Your true soulmate will want you as much as you want them.

Signs that you are not your partner's soulmate

Is it possible to feel a soulmate connection with someone who does not feel the same way for you? One-sided affections are everywhere in life. Here are signs that you are not your partner's soulmate. These points should help you start putting things into perspective.

1. When you are not your partner's soulmate, you end up giving more than you receive.

This implies that you are the one who makes all the moves and acts as though the relationship is essential. They stand back and soak in all the attention while behaving as though they are entitled to the love and attention you shower on them.

2. They have qualities that are a no-nos for you, and they are not willing to work on these; even for you.

In their opinion, you have got to love them the way they are, but they do not hesitate to let you know the things they want you to do and the ways they want you to change for them. And yes, they expect you to do exactly as they say but never return the favor.

3. They feel uncomfortable around you, which continues even as the relationship keeps unfolding.

This discomfort is evident in how they relate with you and their unlikeliness to confide in you or trust what you say to them.

4. They are never satisfied with anything you do.

You are never good enough. You always must try harder; do more to earn their approval and attention; and fit into a predefined character for them to be proud of you. If they could, they would shed you in a heartbeat.

When you notice these points in a relationship, these are indicators that you are not with your soulmate, no matter how strongly you feel about them. The best line of action may be to take a step back.

As much as it is a bitter pill to swallow, soulmate relationships do not always lead to marriage or long-term commitments.

This chapter has been dedicated to opening you up to red flags to look out for when relating to your soulmate. Signs that you are not with your soulmate, and what to do if you discover that your partner is not your soulmate.

I also introduced you to the concept of *change* and showed you what you must do when you notice changes in your partner *(negative changes)*. Make use of this information as you define your relationship's next steps.

Once you internalize that finding your soulmate is no guarantee of success, you can start looking at love realistically and mentally prepare yourself should it fail.

In the final chapter, I want to wrap up all that you've learned about finding your soulmate. You can start to put the action steps in this program into motion this weekend.

See you in the next chapter!

CONCLUSION

Your desire to find and build a stable relationship with your soulmate is commendable. If there is one thing you should know by now; IT IS POSSIBLE.

You may have suffered through a lot in the past. You may have gone through terrible relationships *(or at least relationships that you were not proud of)*. You may have had people laugh at you and tell you that there is no such thing as a *'soulmate,'* but you know better. You will soon prove them wrong.

Your special person is out there, somewhere. And it is your job to position yourself as the kind of person they would want to be with. You must prove to the Universe that you are ready for the blessing of finding and being with your soulmate. Prepare to fight for them and your relationship when you finally meet them.

This program has been a guide to help you through all these steps. And so that these steps remain fresh in your mind, here's a quick recap of the major lessons you have learned in the preceding pages of this blueprint.

1. **You must start your journey to finding your soulmate and true love from a place of finding yourself.**

   You cannot give what you do not have. It will be impossible for you to love your soulmate *(when you finally meet them)* if you have issues loving and accepting yourself. Loving yourself completely is a conscious action and one you must execute before you set out to find your soulmate.

2. **You must let go of the past and become vulnerable.**

   You will not succeed in your quest to find and build forever with your soulmate if you hang on to the mistakes, hurt, and bitterness from the past. Take the past as an incentive to live an ideal present. Reach into the future you deserve; a future of love and happiness with your soulmate.

3. **The Universe is waiting for you and is willing to bring your soulmate your way.**

   This knowledge will help cement in you the consciousness that there is someone out there for you. If you do all you should *(follow through with all the steps discussed in different chapters of this* program*)*, your soulmate will come to you.

4. To find your soulmate, you must be actively involved in the process.

Although the Universe is willing to help you, you must understand that this connection with your soulmate is ultimately the result of a collaborative effort.

You must be willing to do your part and put in the work discussed in the beginning chapters of this program while still holding on to the faith that your soulmate will find you.

5. Timing is everything in this quest to find your soulmate.

It is possible to find your soulmate at the wrong time. If this ever happens to you, the journey to getting together and building a meaningful relationship with them will be difficult *(if not downright impossible)*.

However, you can do a few things to make sure that timing works in your favor. These were discussed in-depth in the 4th chapter of this program.

6. Your soulmate may not come into your life the way you expect.

You may think of your soulmate as royalty who will step into your life to save the day when you are in a dire situation. You may think of them as the holy divine one who will move into the home just across yours this summer.

While these may end up happening for you, it is not always the case. Your soulmate will often come on the scene in the most unconventional ways.

There is every chance that you have met them already, but because you did not know what to look for, this person slipped away from you into the arms of someone else.

Therefore, you must know the signs that show that your soulmate has come into your life. These signs were explained in-depth in the 5th chapter.

7. A beautiful relationship with your soulmate will have its prickly thorns.

Your soulmate is human *(just as you are)*, and to make your relationship work with them, you must commit to it. Challenges will come as the days and months unfold. There will be times when you may be tempted to call it quits and go your separate ways. However, you must learn to make your love work for you.

This is what the 6th chapter of this program taught in detail. Love and your relationship with your soulmate are no walks in the park. Equip yourself with the tips discussed in chapter 6 as you journey to the future you desire.

8. Do not trivialize the subject of physical intimacy with your partner.

This applies to you more if your partner believes that expressing feelings and establishing a deep connection in a relationship requires sexual contact.

Sex is vital, and at the start of your relationship, you may want to have this conversation with your partner.

Please pay attention to what they say, what they do not say, and commit to spicing up your relationship in line with the compromise you reach between yourselves. Chapter 7 discussed the subject of *'sex'* and how it affects your relationship with your soulmate.

9. Change is constant, and we discussed the concept of change in terms of your relationship with your soulmate in chapter 8.

At the beginning of your journey, you dreamed of a loving, attentive partner who enjoys your company. The day you find this person, it feels incredible and somewhat intoxicating.

But have you stopped to think of what will happen if, suddenly, your partner begins to change for the worst? How do you handle the nagging thoughts that keep telling you that your bliss will be short-lived?

How do you ensure that you will build forever with your soulmate and that this relationship will not end up as another conquest you will have to move on from tomorrow?

Nothing is guaranteed in life; not even your relationship with your soulmate. Equip yourself with the strategies for handling changes in yourself and your partner, which was discussed in the last chapter of this program.

My earnest desire is to see you break free from the shackles holding you back from positioning yourself for love. I want that you meet the person of your dreams *(your soulmate)* and build an enviable, long-term relationship with them.

That is why I made this program practical and full of life lessons to apply in your relationship with your soulmate today. Go through this program many times *(so the messages can register in your subconscious)* and begin to work on all action points extracted from these pages.

Above all, believe that you can, and you should - FIND LOVE IN YOUR SOULMATE. Then reach out to the relationship of a lifetime. You deserve the most profound love of your soulmate.

Grab Your FREE Gift on the Next Page

YOUR FREE GIFT

Finding Your Soulmate Tips Sheet

Sometimes you need a quick tip for a situation.
This tips sheet points you to the best resources
to help you fast!
(Get Yours Now...It's FREE)

Request FREE Tips Sheet Today. Go to:
https://loveblueprints.com/soulmate-tips-sheet/

More Books by Christopher Conway

Long Distance Love

eBook | Paperback | Audio Versions
https://loveblueprints.com/long

Finding Your Soulmate

eBook | Paperback | Audio Versions
https://loveblueprints.com/finding

Reference List

Booth, H. (2019, May 20). *"Start low and go slow": how to talk to your partner about sex*. The Guardian. https://www.theguardian.com/lifeandstyle/2019/may/20/start-low-and-go-slow-how-to-talk-to-your-partner-about-sex

Center, R. T. (2019, August 11). *True Love vs. Infatuation*. Restorations Therapy Center. https://www.restorationstherapy.com/true-love-vs-infatuation/

Development, R. (2019, December 1). *Don't date girls who have lots of male friends*. Rebellious Development. https://rebelliousdevelopment.com/dont-date-girls-who-have-male-friends/

Donovan, L. (2014, February 20). *10 Places You Could Meet Your Future Soulmate*.

HelloGiggles. https://hellogiggles.com/lifestyle/10-places-meet-future-soulmate/

Fellizar, K. (2018, October 1). *7 Signs You're Not Actually Your Partner's Soulmate, You're Just Their Type*. Bustle. https://www.bustle.com/p/7-signs-youre-not-actually-your-partners-soulmate-youre-just-their-type-12108991

Gustafson, D. A. L. (2014, May 4). *8 Ways to Grow Love*. HuffPost. https://www.huffpost.com/entry/eight-ways-to-grow-love_b_4894123

Harra, C., & Harra, A. (2016, May 5). *7 Qualities To Seek In A Soulmate*. HuffPost. https://www.huffpost.com/entry/7-qualities-to-seek-in-a-_b_7201494

Kassel, G. (2020, January 24). *6 Reasons Why Sex Is Important in a Relationship*. Well+Good.

https://www.wellandgood.com/why-is-sex-important-relationship/

Kirschner, D. (2020, January 14). *When You Find Your Soulmate at the Wrong Time*. Love in 90 Days. https://lovein90days.com/when-you-find-your-soulmate-at-the-wrong-time/

Laderer, A. (2019, October 18). *How Your Partner's Past Might Impact Your Future*. Talkspace. https://www.talkspace.com/blog/partners-past-impact-your-future/

Laura, V. A. P. B. V. (2019, November 27). *5 Places Where you could Meet your Soulmate*. WordPress.Com. https://valentinalaura.com/2017/08/19/5-places-where-you-could-meet-your-soulmate/

Lawrence, S. (2019, June 10). *3 Signs That You Have Instant Chemistry Because You Loved Each Other In A Past Life*. YourTango. https://www.yourtango.com/experts/sarah-lawrence/how-to-tell-if-you-have-found-love-with-your-soulmate-or-if-its-a-karmic-relationship-from-your-past-life

Leasca, S. (2020, August 24). *13 Best Online Dating Sites to Find Love in 2020*. Glamour. https://www.glamour.com/story/best-online-dating-sites-to-find-love

Leonie, C. (2020, March 9). *Why Some Soulmate Relationships Don't Last*. Caren Reads. https://www.carenreads.com/question-of-the-week-why-some-soulmate-relationships-dont-last-forever/

M. (2020, September 19). *When You Meet Your Soulmate At The Wrong Time*. Thought Catalog. https://thoughtcatalog.com/marissa-hernandez/2015/02/when-you-meet-your-soulmate-at-the-wrong-time/

Mellardo, A. (2017, March 9). *How To Tell If He's Confident, Or Cocky*. Elite Daily. https://www.elitedaily.com/dating/ways-tell-guy-dating-confident-cocky/1819258

Ohlin, B. (2020, November 7). *7 Ways to Improve Communication in Relationships*. PositivePsychology.Com. https://positivepsychology.com/communication-in-relationships/

Positivity, P. O. (2019, May 1). *How to Tell If Your Partner Is Your Soulmate (Or Not)*. Power of Positivity: Positive Thinking & Attitude. https://www.powerofpositivity.com/partner-doesnt-11-qualities-theyre-not-soulmate/

Pugachevsky, J. (2018, May 16). *7 Types Of Bad Men And Why You Keep Dating Them*. Cosmopolitan. https://www.cosmopolitan.com/sex-love/a20159874/how-to-stop-dating-bad-people/

Reid, S. (2016, October 14). *15 Reasons Why You Shouldn't Date A Mama's Boy*. TheTalko. https://www.thetalko.com/15-reasons-why-you-shouldnt-date-a-mamas-boy/

Santoro. (2013, June 30). *Are You Prepared for Love? 5 Ways to Prepare Yourself!* HuffPost. https://www.huffpost.com/entry/finding-love_b_3179023

Schreiber, K. (2016, January 14). *Yes, Being Vulnerable Is Terrifying—But Here's Why It's So Worth It*. Greatist. https://greatist.com/live/fear-of-vulnerability

T. (2018, April 15). *When Soulmates Meet At The Wrong Time - TheLoveWitchProject*. Medium. https://medium.com/@thelovewitchpro/when-soulmates-meet-at-the-wrong-time-2602cb8d19fc

Therapist, T. A. (2018, June 13). *Do you know your love language? (and why it's important)*. Medium. https://angrytherapist.medium.com/do-you-know-your-love-language-and-why-its-important-35c36ab986cc

Understanding Past Relationships. (2020, May 17). Therapy In Philadelphia. https://www.therapyinphiladelphia.com/tips/understanding-past-relationships

Weiss, J. (2017, January 21). *How to Use Your Intuition To Attract Your Soul Mate*. JIM WEISS. https://www.jimweiss.net/use-your-intuition-to-attract-your-soul-mate/

www.ingramcontent.com/pod-product-compliance
Lightning Source LLC
Chambersburg PA
CBHW021445070526
44577CB00002B/261